fridge magnets are bastards

fridge magnets are bastards

an A–Z rant about annoying people and useless things in the modern world

mark dapin

HarperCollinsPublishers

HarperCollins*Publishers*

First published in Australia in 2007
by HarperCollins*Publishers* Australia Pty Limited
ABN 36 009 913 517
www.harpercollins.com.au

HarperCollins*Publishers*
25 Ryde Road, Pymble, Sydney, NSW 2073, Australia
31 View Road, Glenfield, Auckland 10, New Zealand
77–85 Fulham Palace Road, London, W6 8JB, United Kingdom
2 Bloor Street East, 20th floor, Toronto, Ontario M4W 1A8, Canada
10 East 53rd Street, New York NY 10022, USA

National Library of Australia Cataloguing-in-Publication data:

Dapin, Mark.
 Fridge magnets are bastards.
 ISBN 978 0 7322 8521 0 (pbk.).
 1. Middle aged men – Attitudes. 2. Middle aged men – Humor.
 3. Australian wit and humor – 21st century. 4. Popular
 culture – Humor. I Title.
305.261

Cover design by Mark Gowing and Darren Holt
Author photo on back cover courtesy of Fairfax Media
Typeset in 11.5/16.5pt Bembo by Helen Beard, ECJ Australia Pty Limited
Printed and bound in Australia by Griffin Press
79gsm Bulky Paperback used by HarperCollins*Publishers* is a natural, recyclable
product made from wood grown in a combination of sustainable plantation and
regrowth forests. It also contains up to a 20% portion of recycled fibre. The
manufacturing processes conform to the environmental regulations in Tasmania,
the place of manufacture.

5 4 3 2 1   07 08 09 10

To Claire and Ben

And to my mum, who always wanted me to
write a funny book
(maybe next time, eh, Mum?)

An Introduction to Bastardry

This book is an A-to-Z of people and things that are not what they pretend to be (except there is not actually anything listed for 'Y' or 'Z', and the single entry for 'X' is a bit of a stretch). It is a reference work for bastard-spotters, who may be seen standing outside corporate headquarters in all weathers, ticking off the different types of bastard they see in the lobby: the **air-punctuating brand manager**; the large-egoed **CEO**; the **sushi**-eating **marketing guru** etc.

It is also a tool that can be used against bastards. Although there is a season for shooting waterfowl, who never do anybody any harm, there is, incredibly, no season for shooting bastards. Yes, that's right. At no time of the year is it legal to kick down the door of their office, walk past their personal assistant, and fire a shotgun at them. It is, however, perfectly acceptable to beat them to death with this book. Metaphorically speaking, of course.

So, exactly who — or what — is a bastard? Well, it's funny you should ask, since I have here a book I prepared earlier. A bastard is not necessarily somebody who commits acts of infamy: if he were, everybody would be a bastard. We all lie, we all cheat, we all sidle to the back of the bookshop to fart.

At best, bastards impersonate the performance of a function and, at worst, they perform the opposite of that function. **Financial planners**, for instance, pretend to be planning your finances, when they are, in fact, using your finances to plan theirs.

In these pages, I will use a great deal of parenthesis and a few footnotes. I will repeatedly employ the (a) and (b) form, because (a) it lends a spurious academic feel to the material; and (b) I think it is kind of funny. I will draw largely on my own experiences, and I will usually locate myself or a conversation 'in the pub'. This is not the apocryphal 'pub' so often referred to by bastards, but an actually existing pub, usually in Sydney or Melbourne, occasionally in Perth or London.

I will speak with a deceptive sense of intimacy about people I hardly know or — in the case of Paris Hilton — I have never met. I will call them by their first names, even though they would never recognise mine.

I shall mostly refer to bastards as 'he', even though bastards are equally represented among both sexes. There are gay bastards, straight bastards and bi-curious bastards. Oddly, there seem to be rather more short bastards than tall bastards, but it will be of no surprise to anyone to learn there is a large contingent of fat bastards. Rich bastards outnumber poor bastards because many forms of bastardry are inherently profitable.

And not all bastards are people. Some are **fridge magnets**, for instance.

Not everybody who looks like a bastard is a bastard, but there are a few simple clues that will lead the bastard-spotter to correctly identify his or her quarry. Most bastards exhibit certain behaviours which, while not unique to their species, are nonetheless characteristic.

If they are women, they might screech when they meet another woman they haven't seen for a long time — about an hour, say — and hug them. If they are men, they usually wear a suit and tie.

Of course, not every man in a suit is a bastard. Some are ordinary, decent blokes on their way to defend themselves in court. And not every woman who yells at an acquaintance is evil. They may simply be screaming with fear at the sight of a screeching bastard racing towards them with open arms.

A useful way of identifying a bastard is to count the number of people it takes to do his job. Bastards often have assistants to answer their phones, write in their diaries, collect their dry-cleaning, have sex with them etc. They also appoint deputies to perform the few tasks required of them at work that cannot decently be avoided. A bastard's area of competence is generally so tiny, he can do nothing for himself. Even when he plays **golf**, the so-called 'sport of bastards', he has caddies to fetch and carry for him.

Not all bastards are bad people and not all bad people are bastards. Pauline Hanson, for instance, is a racist but she is among the least bastardly of all extreme right-wingers, most of whom secretly believe the Jews use UFOs to control the weather. Hanson simply dislikes foreigners, especially those Aussies-come-lately, the Aborigines. More accurately, she dislikes foreignness, and thinks it belongs overseas.

I once asked Pauline the meaning of the term **unAustralian**.

'Multiculturalism is unAustralian,' she told me. 'Australians don't mind kids coming here as long as they want to be Australian, to learn the language. It's unAustralian to hear this foreign language.'

Which foreign language?

'Well, any foreign language.'

Foreign language is unAustralian?

'Well, *it is*,' insisted Pauline. 'English is the language here.'

These are not the weasel words of a bastard. They are the firmly held convictions of an **idiot**.

The attorney general **Philip Ruddock** is neither a racist nor an idiot, but he is a bastard — not because he sends asylum seekers to Nauru, but because he does so while wearing an Amnesty International badge.

In writing this book, I have several times found myself nodding my head in agreement with my own wise words, and I trust you will, too. If you do not, you are probably a bastard.

advertorial

noun, 1. advertising content in magazines and newspapers, designed to look like editorial. **2.** bollocks

People expect the content of media to be divided into:

Editorial: news, features and opinion, written to entertain and inform by journalists who can say whatever they like except when it clashes with the interests of their billionaire proprietors or any of their proprietors' billionaire friends.

Advertising: text and images contrived by **creatives** contracted by corporations to make ludicrous claims about products that are manufactured by death-row prisoners in Chinese jails.

Advertising, on paper and on the air, is directly paid for by advertisers, and only **idiots** and former Liberal Senator **Santo Santoro** believe it. Editorial is not directly paid for by advertisers and, although many **media cynics** affect a vast suspicion of journalism, it is their only source of knowledge of the world outside of their immediate experience.

The task of the advertising and marketing departments of newspapers and magazines is to blur the distinction between advertising and editorial to such an extent that, when readers come across an ad, they are coaxed into believing it is a neutral endorsement of a product.

If a product is useful and popular, magazines and newspapers will often promote it for nothing in feature stories and reviews. It will become the Next Big Thing, until the next big thing. If its utility, quality or supremacy over similar products in the marketplace is not immediately apparent, the product may have to rely on an advertising campaign, featuring a beguiling slogan over an appealing image that contrives to suggest that the buyer will quickly find themselves having sex with suntanned blond people.

If, however, it is absolutely useless — if, for instance, it is a homeopathic bowel-cleansing serum, or the life of Elvis Presley retold on limited-edition commemorative dinner plates — the manufacturer has to resort to advertorial to try to trick people into buying it. A useful way of gauging if a product is any good is to count the number of words used to advertise it and compare the total with the length of the nearest story.

If the ad comprises only a tagline and some very little words at the bottom, the product is probably legitimate but the price is vastly underquoted. As the small print will explain, the figure given is exclusive of, for instance, all applicable taxes and surcharges (if it is an airfare), flights (if it is an overseas holiday) or wheels (if it is a car). Alternatively, it may be the price for only one person when the product (a hotel room, car hire) etc has to be purchased by two. This is known as 'clever **marketing**', widely considered an oxymoron outside of the marketing 'profession'.

If the ad contains a large block of text and small picture of a man wearing a white coat, who looks like a doctor, then the product is partially fraudulent, and definitely costs almost nothing to make and an enormous amount to market. The 'doctor' is almost certainly a doctor of philosophy. If there is a facsimile of his signature at the bottom of the ad, he probably got his PhD over the internet.

If there are more words in the ad than in the average feature story, and those words are printed in the same typeface as the story, across the same column measure, and written in a way that suggests an arthropod is attempting to write passionate, pithy magazine journalism, then you are reading advertorial and you can be certain that the product does not work.

air punctuation

***noun,* 1.** twat hats

Unless I'm much mistaken — and it would not be the first time[1] — the cancer of air punctuation did not die out in the last cull of very stupid people. If anything, the passage of the years appears to have made it stronger.

Air punctuation is the use in conversation of a simultaneous wiggle of the index and middle fingers to represent inverted commas. When I first saw this digital dance performed in public, I assumed it was a gang sign indicating membership of the unproductive professions: advertising, **marketing**, **public relations**, **human resources** and **consultancy**.

The practitioners of these dubious arts are given to the early adoption of new words, phrases, mannerisms and beliefs. To help them get through their working days without committing themselves to anything, they have evolved a language of their own, which uses words simply to make noise. They say things like '**marketing** is "the means by which mutually beneficial exchanges occur"', or **life coaching** is 'a collaborative solution-focused, results-orientated and systematic process in which the coach facilitates the enhancement of work, performance, life experience, self-directed learning and personal growth of the coachee', and sit back and smile like the Buddha, as if they have passed on a universal truth.

The destruction of the spoken language alone was never

---

[1] It would, in fact, be the fifth time.

going to satisfy their desire to rule the world by avoiding the issues. They had to attack punctuation, too.

Punctuation is a rare and wonderful thing.[1] Without it, sentences would go on forever, quotations would languish unattributed, and nuance would be lost. The beauty of punctuation is that it is an unseen servant of the speaker. It signals its existence in the natural pauses and breaks in conversation. Bastards could not stand this, so they invented air punctuation, making inverted commas visible by wiggling their middle and index fingers on either side of their head, often accompanied by a raising of the eyebrows or rolling of the eyes.

I have identified five ways in which bastards use visible inverted commas. I call them 'The Five Ways in which Bastards Use Visible Inverted Commas'™.

(1) To flag an intentional irony. Eg 'I'm really [wiggles fingers] happy [wiggles fingers] to be kept outside the **loop**.'

(2) In place of the words 'so-called'. Eg 'He's an [wiggles fingers] intellectual [wiggles fingers].'

(3) To demonstrate their disagreement with a particular concept. Eg 'He's trying to [wiggles fingers] change the world [wiggles fingers].'

(4) To show that they have heard other people use the words before. Eg 'We have to formulate our corporate response to [wiggles fingers] global warming [wiggles fingers].'

(5) No reason at all. Some bastards are just addicted to air punctuation.

---

[1] With the single exception of the rowdy, intrusive and generally redundant exclamation mark which, until the invention of sky quotes, was the bastard's favoured punctuation. Even today, bastards think nothing of closing a sentence with three, five or six exclamation marks!!!!

One thing you can be certain of, however, is they never actually use them as fucking *quotation marks*. They never say, for instance, 'As Winston Churchill said [wiggles fingers], "We will fight them on the beaches [wiggles fingers]."'

Readers may be surprised to learn that I am not, by training, an evolutionary biologist. However, I had assumed that natural selection would deal with air punctuation. When the bastard raises his fingers in an apparent gesture of wiggly surrender, he is robbed of his natural defences, and invites a punch on the nose. I thought concussion would claim the air punctuator, and he would go the way of other extinct corporate types such as the bottom-pincher and the flip-chart guy.

But no. The practice has multiplied beyond the ranks of the unproductive professions and into the world of ordinary, decent people. It must be stopped before it spreads to other punctuation marks, and people begin bending at the waist to show a question, flipping one foot to denote a pause, or pulling off their head and jumping on it to indicate an exclamation.

availability

noun, **1.** an attribute of thermo-dynamic function

Although human beings might be available to do something, they cannot actually 'have' availability. To suggest they do reduces them to something less than data. The term 'availability' exists primarily in physics — but also in computer science, systems engineering and navigation — and has no application to human relations.

Bastard-busting tip number one: When a bastard asks 'What is your availability tomorrow morning?' say, 'My availability is the difference between the enthalpy per unit mass of substance and the product of entropy per unit mass multiplied by the lowest temperature available to me for heat discard tomorrow morning.'

backmasker

noun, 1. really scary devil worshipper

Evangelical Christians in the 1980s were consumed by the idea that certain rock records contained Satanic messages recorded backwards that impressionable young people would hear and then act upon. **Queen**'s rubbish single *Another One Bites the Dust* is famous for two reasons. It is the most often cited example of backmasking, and it was the record chosen by one British radio DJ to play out the announcement of Freddie Mercury's death. Backwards, it said, 'Decide to smoke marijuana, it's fun to smoke marijuana.' Apparently. The Eagles' *Hotel California* is an unpopular song with Christians even when it's played the right way around. Anton Le Vey, founder of the Church of Satan, is pictured on the inside cover of the album sleeve and the lyrics are held to refer to all kinds of devilish goings on. Backwards, it is much the same story, with the message, 'Yes, Satan, he organised his own religion… it was delicious. He puts it in a vat.' But if there is one band the fundamentalists hate more than the Eagles, it is Led Zeppelin. Curiously, this is not because their songs go on for hours and hours without getting anywhere, or because their lyrics are a load of meaningless hippy drivel, but because Jimmy Page bought celebrity Satanist Aleister Crowley's house in Scotland, and because *Stairway to Heaven* backwards says, 'I live for Satan… The Lord turns me off… There's no escaping it… Here's to my sweet Satan.'

Back at home, Wagga Wagga musician Ray Keuning, a follower of the Church of Christ, complained to the Australian Broadcasting Tribunal when he played the Bicentennial jingle *Celebration of a Nation* backwards and discovered the words, 'How about it, Satan, he is master of sex, he and I will wash heaven and make it great. Let him possess the one leader.' Ray had submitted 13 other backwards TV ads to the ABT, all of them containing messages from Satan.

While most of the mainstream examples of backmasking appear to be elaborate fantasies on behalf of the non-listener, the fake backmasking craze brought about a real backmasking backlash, and champion death metal bands actually did add backwards messages to their brilliant recordings. Who can forget Slayer's backwards 'join us' (Ooh! Scary!) or Cradle of Filth's backwards *Lord's Prayer*? Well, anybody can, because even CD players don't play backwards.

badge

noun, **1. fridge magnet** for a jacket

bagel, non-boiled

noun, **1.** bread

There are too many bagels around these days, and many of them are impostors. Bagels should be bought after midnight on a winter's evening from a Russian emigrant with a five-syllable name and a thousand-year-old face. They should be hard and heavy, like life in the old country. They should be round with a hole in the middle. Most of all, they should be boiled before they are baked.

Bagels are the saving grace of my Jewish childhood memory, which is otherwise populated by frightening relatives, looming initiation ceremonies and learning Hebrew by rote. The bagel is a rare treat that is a staple food, something nice that is encouraged. It is low in fat and contains no cholesterol. It is not a funny-shaped bread roll.

If the dough is not boiled before it is baked, the 'bagel' is not a Jewish bagel. It is, in fact, anti-Semitic. Since the boiling process accounts for 60 per cent of the cost of making the bagel, most places simply set their dough on a rack oven and steam it. Many bakeries that claim to have boiled bagels are simply calling steaming 'boiling', a clear act of bastardry. A bagel must have a crusty outer skin and a chewy interior.

The bagel became a victim of its own popularity, not a fate commonly associated with Jewish stuff. It is a symptom of the decline of the artisan baker that non-Jewish bagels abound, doughy affronts to a proud heritage. Airy and insubstantial, the non-Jewish bagel is often an option in city sandwich bars, along with non-Italian focaccia and non-Turkish Turkish bread.

The EU has regulations about this kind of thing. Champagne cannot be called champagne unless it is made from grapes grown in the Champagne region. Chiko Rolls cannot be called Chiko Rolls unless it can be proven that a Chiko died horribly to produce them. The same stringent laws should apply to bagels in Australia. For a bagel to bear the proud name of its crusty, chewy forefathers, it should be boiled. And any bastard who tries to sell a bread roll with a hole in the middle as a bagel should be boiled alive, too.

baldness

noun, **1.** a biological condition designed to make charming, intelligent, older men feel unattractive to younger women

There is no good reason why men — specifically, me — should go bald as they grow older. Hair is not a burden that needs to be shed, or a passing torment of youth, like acne. Yet it has been suggested that I am indeed losing my hair. It certainly seems that there is a lot less of it than there was five years ago, or five months ago, or even five days ago. Hair has fled my crown completely, leaving a barren area the width of a skullcap and the shape of a crop circle. At the same time, my fringe appears to be retreating to the back of my head. I can imagine a time in the near future (about 10.55pm tonight) when baldness will have blazed a broad, direct path from my forehead to the crop circle, forming an integrated runway and landing pad for very small flying saucers. Yet I have convinced myself that if I have my hair cut very short, it will look like I have more of it. (I read this once in a magazine.)

Bald men fear women will not want to have sex with them, in the same way that men don't generally want to have sex with bald women. Therefore, baldness drives men to make strange and terrible grooming decisions, such as growing compensatory facial hair, coaxing a comb-over, or wearing a ridiculous hat. Male pattern baldness — a genetically determined condition — affects about 66 per cent of all men at some time in their lives. Chains of self-styled clinics typically offer them laser treatments, strand-by-strand transplants, scalp reduction surgery, creams, wigs or any combination of the above. An average 'treatment' costs about $10,000. In 2002, Advanced Hair Studio calculated the industry in Australia was worth about $200 million a year.

This is a ludicrous allocation of resources. Why isn't *more* money spent on searching for a solution to this scourge? It seems scientists can put a man on the moon, but they cannot put hair on his head. It is time to take the problem out of the hands of boffins and pass it on to the only people who can really do something about it: the international rock-star community. Twice, they have saved the Third World from famine, now it is time they turned their attentions to the First World, where people actually buy their records (or, at least download their songs). Surely, a bald Bob Geldof — a role that could perhaps be played by our own Peter Garrett — could harass and harangue the world's increasing population of bald rockers to form a bald supergroup to record a ballad entitled *We are the Bald*, which would finally and conclusively put an end to world baldness forever. I see Michael Stipe from REM singing a duet with Sinead O'Connor, while Angry Anderson **gnomes** around in the background.

If you are unfairly struck with both male pattern baldness and myopia, it is strongly advised that you resist the temptation to express your individuality by growing a beard.

My brother used to fill long hours on dreary weekends in provincial England playing 'Baldhead, Beard and Glasses'. The game involved spotting a man with all three attributes in a public place, shouting 'Baldhead, beard and glasses!' and taking his photograph.

My brother acquired hundreds of pictures of short-sighted blokes whose hair grew — inexplicably, it seemed at the time — at the wrong end of their heads. They looked surprised, they looked guilty, they looked annoyed but — most of all — they looked exactly the same.

In mid-2007, long after Baldhead, Beard and Glasses had been abandoned for other, less physically exacting pursuits, my brother and I were sitting in a hotel, slowly balding.

'What if you could have all your hair back,' he said, suddenly, 'but your ears grew an inch?'

I thought for a moment.

'No,' I said. 'I'd have the biggest ears in the world.'

Cruel people would post pictures of me on their websites. Children in the street would shout 'Spock!' and 'Where's Noddy?' In the winter months, I would have to wear little woolly ear-caps, of a type not yet invented, but that I imagine would look a bit like the hats on racks of lamb. Also, the boy with the second-biggest ears in the world would beat me up on the way to work.

'Okay,' he said, 'what if you could have all your hair back, but you lost your little finger?'

Sure. Who needs fingers? Our childhood mate Paul, who lost a digit in an unlikely accident with a 19th-century ship's cannon, used it as a chat-up line.

'Would you like to see me wiggle my stump?' he would ask never-particularly-innocent young women, usually as a prelude to punching their boyfriends in the face with his incomplete fist.

My brother agreed that he would trade one finger for one million hair follicles, although I suspect the exchange rate will plummet in the years to come, probably reaching parity by 2026, when — at the current rate of attrition — we will only have one hair each as a souvenir of our never-particularly-hirsute youth.

'Would you eat a live cockroach for a million dollars?' I asked him.

'I'd do it for $10,000,' he said.

After a short burst of vigorous bargaining, I got him down to $1250.

This surprised me because (a) I would eat a cockroach to save myself from something worse — growing bigger ears, perhaps — but not for financial reward; and (b) insects are not a regular part of my brother's strictly regulated diet, which traditionally has largely drawn nutrition from two sources: confectionery and nicotine.

Although my brother admitted he might eat a live spider 'for a laugh', he was unsure whether he would accept a million dollars to eat cheese. (There is no cheese in my brother's diet, because he was once made to eat cheese in a home-economics lesson at school, and he subsequently threw up.) Finally, he decided he would take the million, if he was allowed soft-cheese triangles as (literally) his poison.

Tragically, however, we both agree we would eat cockroach-and-spider omelette with all the trimmings, if only we could grow back our hair. And keep our ear size stable.

ballet

***noun*, 1.** highly unpopular art form

Although some bastards pretend to like ballet, this is a lot less common than feigning an appreciation for **opera**, because ballet is a form of dance. Most male Australians like dancing to look like two people having sex with their clothes on, whereas most ballet troupes like dancing to look like a mime artist doing yoga on ice skates. The majority of bastards, therefore, think ballet is a bit girly, and pretending to like it does not suit their curious self image as phallic, thrusting military leaders (see **corporate warriors**).

Ballet is often derided as old-fashioned, although attempts were made to update it in the early 1980s, with lopsided haircuts and diagonally buttoned shirts. This was called 'Spandau Ballet', after Rudolf Hess, the prisoner of Spandau, an unrepentant Nazi bastard.

ball-park figure

***noun*, 1.** thoughtlessly applied American sporting analogy, referring to an approximate number

Bastard-busting tip number two: Nurture a knowledge of baseball. When a bastard asks you to name a ball-park figure, shout, 'Babe Ruth!'

beard

***noun*, 1. fridge magnet** for a face

Before he became prime minister, former British Labour Party leader Tony Blair told his shadow frontbench to shed their facial hair as they had shed their socialism. It was one more signal that he would stop at nothing to achieve power. Always an astute and clean-cut populist, Tony knows that voters do not trust bearded politicians. Australia has not had a bearded prime minister since Joseph Cook in 1913.

The clean-shaven masses have always suspected their bearded brethren of hiding more than just a weak bone structure behind their woolly chin curtains. From 1914, beards were seen as a sign of cowardliness: troops in World War I had to shave to prevent trench lice — a hirsute face signalled a man who hadn't enlisted.

Biologists believe the beard, like the pubic hair it so closely resembles, is a sign of sexual availability. However, a recent English poll showed that 65 per cent of women prefer a clean-shaven man.

Employers do not like beards. In a survey by London management consultant Aziz Corporation, 27 per cent of businessmen said beards looked 'untidy' and almost a quarter of bearded businessmen thought their beards put them at a disadvantage.

Former biochemist Christine Dunn, later of Professional Image Consultancy in Melbourne, has studied the scientific meaning of facial hair. 'Basically, a moustache is a penis and a full beard means hiding,' she says. 'I've noticed that when men have a crisis in their sex life, they sometimes grow a moustache. Then, when things come good again, they cut it off. When they have a crisis generally, they'll grow a beard.

'I always advise my clients to cut off facial hair. It puts up a barrier and says, "You're not allowed to look at me." Also, in our society there's the idea that maybe they're hiding a weak chin, which will give away their character.'

For a couple of years, I lived with a bearded flatmate. I didn't have a DVD player, a video, or even a TV, so I occupied myself with an energetic but ultimately futile campaign to persuade him to shave off his beard. He lived a good-natured, hairy existence in the privacy of his room, shelling cigarettes like peas and exploring the farthest reaches of the internet, which was then young and vibrant and bursting with free farmyard porn.[1]

Looking back, they seem like idyllic days, although they were probably just idle. We had a dishwasher but it was never turned on, because I did not know how to use it and I didn't cook anyway. My flatmate didn't even eat. He appeared to be a self-sustaining life-form, perhaps obtaining his nutrients through photosynthesis, or feeding off the thousands of tiny organisms that inhabited his beard. Perhaps he clung to his beard — or, more accurately, his beard clung to him — for that very reason.

However, I felt I had a moral obligation to free him from his curly chains. A close friend of mine had worn a beard from his late teens to his mid-20s, and found it acted as a cheap and reliable form of contraception.

As soon as he went clean shaven — although, in the manner of most reforming beardies, he hung onto his moustache for a while — his luck changed. Girls no longer feared the 'Velcro effect' during intimate moments.

'Why didn't you *tell* me?' he asked.

---

[1] This is not to suggest my flatmate was looking for farmyard porn.

I resolved that if I ever had another bearded mate, I would do what I could to save him from himself. But my flatmate refused to be saved, and eventually managed to get himself into a relationship despite his beard.

Bluebeard, Blackbeard and my mates' beards notwithstanding, the history of the beard has not been entirely infamous. Founding fathers such as Henry Parkes wore beards, as did John Pascoe Fawkner, founder of Melbourne, George Robertson, founder of Angus & Robertson, and the founders of most other things. Growing beards and establishing institutions once went hand-in-hand, but it has been some time since a bearded innovator has come up with anything more socially useful than a murderous cult.

Reginald Reynolds, author of *Beards, An Omnium Gatherum*, published in 1950, revealed four truths about beards:

(1) That not all are given beards, though all are born with noses;

(2) That beards appear to originate from an accident of sex, though some women have produced them;

(3) That they may be worn to conceal a sorry countenance, though not prohibited to persons with well-cast features;

(4) That there is no discernible evidence for the view that bearded men are more addicted than others to the eating of horseflesh.

The lesson is clear. While the Australian Labor Party might take the razor to its commitment to economic rationalism, it will only win an election by washing its whiskers down the sink. Otherwise, its candidates will be seen as shifty, weak-chinned accidents who may or may not eat horses.

For further information on facial foliage, see **Appendix A: The 13 Types of Beard.**

beazley

adverb, **1.** repeatedly unsuccessfully. Eg He stood for prime minister three times beazley. **2.** with manufactured outrage. Eg He attacked the government's record over Iraq beazley, and pretended he would not have done the same thing himself. **3.** with detrimental effect on the organisation to which he/she belongs. Eg He led the Labor Party beazley. **4.** weakly, without conviction. Eg He led the Labor Party beazley. **5.** to defeat. Eg He led the Labor Party beazley

In 2006, Kim Beazley finally stepped down as leader after 116 years in the Australian Labor Party. His first political position was as the ghost gum, or 'Tree of Knowledge', under which striking sheep shearers founded the ALP in Barcaldine, Queensland in 1891. Subsequently, he made great use of the tree-like qualities of woodenness, bulk and the ability to shed his bark annually.

Kim Beazley is a member of the Kim Beazley family of Kim Beazleys. His father, the imaginatively named Kim Beazley, was the education minister who abolished university fees in the Gough Whitlam government. Kim Beazley II was a defence, education and transport minister under Bob Hawke, who may initially have mistaken him for a beer fridge. Like most sequels, the second Kim Beazley was not as good as the first one and, like the *Star Wars* movie that was named the worst follow-up ever by E! Online, he posed only a phantom menace to his opponents.

Kim Beazley quickly rose through the ranks of the ALP due to his undoubted ability to quickly rise through the ranks of the

ALP. When Mark Latham was forced to resign the Labor leadership in January 2005, due to a 'life-threatening illness' that does not appear to have killed him yet, Kim won the leadership for an unprecedented 274th time.

Under Kim's leadership, there was never any doubt where he stood, largely because of his imposing bulk. It was, however, less than clear what he stood for. One of his finest political initiatives was his suggestion that people who come to Australia should be presented with an Australian 'values' statement on their visa, and be 'required to sign off on those values' before they are allowed into the country. Any tourist who did not believe in fair play could go to a place where that particular abstraction is not valued, such as **Saudi Arabia**, our unflinching ally in the **War on Terror**. Except that individual tourists are not allowed in Saudi Arabia.

Kim finally came unstuck during the 'Rovegate' scandal, in which he accidentally said 'Karl Rove' when he meant 'Rove McManus'. This threw into doubt everything he had ever said about anything. How could a man who could not distinguish between Roves — especially when one had been married to the late Belinda Emmett and the other had never even been out with her — be trusted to tell Iraq from Iran, Turkey from Turkmenistan, or weapons of mass destruction from trailers for manufacturing hydrogen for weather balloons?

When Kim was finally unseated by some bloke who wears glasses, even *The Economist*, the international newspaper of the bossing classes, was moved to comment he 'consistently fared badly in the polls, because he has been unable to explain how, or indeed if, Labor differs from the conservatives'.

best practice

noun, 1. nothing; just something to say. Eg 'Blah blah blah best practice blah blah blah'

black armband theory of history

noun, 1. a theory of history based on generally acknowledged historical facts, popular with 'basket weavers' etc. **2.** a very bad theory of history indeed

Recently, there has been sustained interest in the black armband theory of history, led by the prime minister John Howard. It is unusual for a head of state to concern himself with the methodology and interpretation of historiography — particularly a hitherto unknown branch of the discipline apparently identified by a single conservative academic, Geoffrey Blainey — but at least it took voters' minds off the war in Iraq.

Proponents of the black armband theory of history believe Aboriginal people were living in Australia when the British arrived. They say they were massacred by convict settlers, and some settlers were actually hanged for their crimes. They say Aboriginal soldiers fought in every Australian war, but it was not until 1962 that all Aboriginal people won the right to vote in Commonwealth elections (and 1965 that they were able to vote in Queensland state elections) and that, even at that time, it remained illegal to encourage them to enrol. They say many Aboriginal farm workers were largely paid in sugar, butter and tobacco, until the Pastoral Industry Award of 1968. They know the names of the unpaid workers and the properties where they worked. The extremists among them even claim that it was the British who brought alcohol to Australia.

Opponents of the black armband theory believe that all this stuff about dates and places and names and votes and slave labour and the British brewing the grog is a smokescreen cynically put in place to deliberately obscure the broader sociological truth that Aboriginal disadvantage is all their own fault, because they are a bunch of work-shy bludgers who drink too much.

box, thinking outside the

noun, 1. a stupid idea put forward by someone with no experience in the field in which he is working — for instance, a consultant. Eg After Islamist hijackers flew passenger jets into the World Trade Center, George Bush invaded the only secular nation in the Middle East. George was thinking outside the box

brand

noun, **1.** word used by bastards when they mean 'thing'. **2.** word used by bastards when they mean 'nothing' (eg 'This is our brand manager' = This man does nothing. 'I care **passion**ately about the brand' = I don't care about anything)

breakfast TV host

noun, **1.** hangover-proof android

I never used to watch breakfast TV, and was mildly surprised to learn that it still existed, but the birth of my son introduced me to the many delights of the early morning. Get this, for instance: there are some people who are awake while it is still dark. A small minority of these lunatics work for TV companies, and they have staff who scour the country searching for other people who are awake, so the breakfast TV host can interview them in the studio.

Breakfast TV hosts are like the officious, cheerful relative who bustles around your living room in the morning, cleaning up the bottles, bodies and bucket bongs from the night before. Even though she is helping, you wish she was not there, or that she would at least have the bad grace to be miserable.

I have not actually seen the beginning of a breakfast TV show

— they could be on all night, for all I know — but by the time I get up, most of the hosts are flirting with each other furiously. Why do they look so smug? Are they wearing butt plugs? Why don't they ever get hangovers? Are they **teetotallers**? What time do they go to bed? Just after *Play School*? Why do they always banter as if they were only a bottle of Dom and half a dozen oysters away from jumping into bed with each other? If they really wanted to have sex with other people, why did they get a job that involved getting up during the *Guthy-Renker Hour*? Has the early-to-bed/early-to-rise routine made them healthy, wealthy and wise, as advertised? It does not seem to have done much to develop the intelligence of the people who do the weather, for instance. How do they get their hair to stay in place? Are they wearing rubber heads? And what do the studio guests think of dragging themselves out of bed to talk to a pair of flirting, grinning, butt-plugged, sculpted-haired presenters, who might at any minute take off their shirts and dance around the weather map in coconut bras?

I guess I'll never find out, because they're not likely to invite me on the show to promote this book now.

bumper sticker

noun, **1.** fridge magnet for a car

Hey, burnout boy! Do you really think fat chicks are clamouring to climb into the back of your shitbox ute? Or that you'd really turn them away if they were?

bush poet

noun, **1. beard**ed clown who writes verse in the style of Banjo Paterson, but crap

It takes more than a hat to make a bushie, and it takes more than rhyme to make a poet. Your poems are useless, mate. Give up.

C

call centre

noun, 1. group of young Indians marked by their distinctive costume of Akubra hats, Driza-Bone coats and Blundstone boots, even though it's 40 degrees in the shade

I recently had a call from a call centre. A recorded voice told me I had been placed on hold, and asked me to wait for the first available operator. I put the phone down, so I don't know what they wanted, but I doubt they were trying to ask me out for a drink — and, even if they were, the cost of flying to Kolkata would negate any saving I might make on a bottle of Cobra Beer and a bowl of peanuts.

I feel sorry for call-centre operators. Apparently, they get a lot of abuse from callers who are angry that Australian jobs have been outsourced to Indians and people who live in Adelaide. As a result, the sub-continentals have hit on the endearing strategy of pretending not to be Indian. In the last year or so, their accents have become perceptively more ocker, and their vocabulary has been enriched with a kind of picture-postcard 'Strine, as if they had been given a seminar on Australian manners by bushmen who had disappeared from the country decades ago — the Leyland Brothers, maybe.

I was prepared for a typically futile exchange with my PC helpline, when a consultant answered the phone affecting a strange Crocodile Mumbai, Indo-Australian drawl, and distinguished himself by wishing me a happy Anzac Day. It was the first time anybody has ever wished me a happy Anzac Day — and, perhaps, the first time anybody had wished anybody a happy Anzac Day — but at least it was, in fact, Anzac Day. Sadly, he blew his cover when he ended the call by inviting me to have a good evening, when it was only 9.30am.

I like to imagine these beleaguered young graduates sitting in offices decorated like outback theme pubs, surrounded by yellow road signs reading 'Platypus crossing' and 'Beware of koala bears', and taking their toilet breaks in portaloos with 'Rules of the Dunny' stuck up behind the door.

It is a rule of call centres that, no matter how simple your request, the first consultant you speak to will not be qualified to handle your call. You must, however, tell them your entire life story before they can make that judgment. What's your date of birth? What's your address? What's your mother's maiden name, for God's sake.

Once they have gathered all this information, they realise that they're only the receptionist, and transfer you to another department, where another receptionist asks you the same questions before passing you on to a consultant, who finds it difficult to tell what might be wrong with your laptop because you are in a serviced apartment in Surfers Paradise and he is in the Ettamogah Hotel in Uttar Pradesh.

Tempers become quickly frayed because you only dial a call centre in times of extreme stress, such as when your hard drive has crashed, you have lost your credit card, or you can't get the name of a phone-sex company off your family phone bill.

At times like these, it does not help that you can hardly understand the technical-support person because your first language is English and he keeps saying things like, 'Strewth, cobber! Sounds like yer bloody computer's got a few roos lose in its top paddock!'

When I was trying to receive messages on my new mobile phone, the call-centre worker asked which company supplied my email. I told her it was AAPT.

'Is that the American Association of Physics Teachers?' she replied.

No, I said, it is one of the largest providers of telecommunications services in the world.

She did not believe there was any such company as AAPT — and, in India, there may not be. I gave up and put down the phone. I am still waiting for her to call me back. In fact, maybe that was her on the line the other day.

candle shop

***noun*, 1.** superfluous main-street retailer, whose supplier, for inexplicable reasons, secreted himself with the butcher and the baker inside a potato

Every time I walk to the supermarket to buy sausages, I am confronted by the perplexing presence of a shop that would seem to have no natural constituency. The first time I noticed it, I read its signboard advertising 'green tea candles' and chuckled to myself, thinking the writer must have missed out the comma between 'tea' and 'candles'.

In fact, the shop really does stock green-tea candles — and every other type of candle, too. I can think of a number of retailers we need in the area — a speciality sausage shop, for instance — but I wouldn't have thought there were many instances when local people had to dash out and buy a candle. The electrification of urban Australia was completed soon after the Great Patriotic War, and the candle-making industry had long since been devastated by the invention of the paraffin lamp.

Of course, there are still some people who do not have electric light, primarily that noble band of prophets who store their possessions in bin liners and push them around the city in shopping trolleys. However, these folk do not, as a rule, live near speciality candle shops.

The other day, I was dawdling vacantly outside the supermarket when I noticed the candle-shop signboard touting its 'autumn/winter collection now in store'.

I don't know why the design of a winter candle should differ from a summer candle — although it is possible, I guess, that winter candles give off more light and heat, and therefore need broader wicks. The distinction between an autumn candle and spring candle is even more inscrutable.

It is sad that the kind of **creative** mind that can come up with a green-tea candle cannot be put to more practical use in a world crying out for an invisibility-reversal spray for missing **elephants**; a deadset cure for **baldness**; and, most of all, low-fat chicken curry sausages.

Carr

proper noun, **1.** Carr, Bob; former Labor premier of New South Wales, now fighting for social democracy at Macquarie Bank. *noun,* **2.** any person or object that acts in a similar manner to Bob Carr, eg 'to park one's Carr'; to move to a more convenient position that is apparently opposite your previous position, eg to move from the Australian Labor Party to Macquarie Bank. *adverb,* **3.** 'to bob Carr'; to bounce around freely

For many years, Handsome Bob Carr was premier of NSW and leader of the NSW ALP, a political party — largely funded by property developers — active in the NSW Parliament (where it is opposed by the NSW Liberal Party, a political party largely funded by property developers).

As might be expected, a lot of property got developed on the ALP's watch, including the beautiful 'Toaster' building, East Circular Quay, which serves the dual purpose of providing much-needed housing for battlers such as Alan Jones (who had denounced the structure as a 'monstrosity' when he did not live there) and shielding from public view the eyesore of the Royal Botanical Gardens.

Bob was widely considered a political intellectual, measured by the traditional Australian yardstick that he wore glasses. One of his brainiest political initiatives was the decision to send **sniffer dogs** into pubs, so as to frighten away drug dealers, cats etc, and make refugees from brutal Third World dictatorships feel more at home. Since **teetotaller** Bob did not use pubs himself, he may have mistaken them for crack houses.

Bob's other contribution to the science of criminology was made as leader of the Opposition, when he put forward the theory that you could spot teenage gang members by the fact they wore their baseball caps backwards. (This was in 1994, when only truck-driving serial killers wore their hats the right way around.) Honest Bob denied making the link, but his policy document clearly described gangs as 'youths, their baseball hats turned back-to-front' and proposed to ban 'emblems and colours which promote gangs' from schools.

Members of the Young Labor Left highlighted Bob's meticulous piece of social observation by attending the State ALP Conference with their caps tilted in the offending fashion, and not murdering anybody.

'Let's ban short-sighted, headline-grabbing policies instead,' Young Labor Leftist Emma Maiden suggested.

'If you are saying to me that gangs have a place in the school system, you can start thinking again,' blustered Bob, intelligently.

Everyone remembers where they were at the moment Bob announced his resignation from politics, on 27 July 2005. I was in the pub with the bloke who used to be Predator on the TV show *Gladiators*.[1]

Of course, Bob quickly went on to become a part-time consultant for merchant bankers Macquarie Bank, the de facto government of Australia and owner of most of our national infrastructure. His parting gift to NSW was Sydney's Cross-City Tunnel, a wildly expensive underground road that nobody uses, but which takes business away from the colourful transsexual prostitutes on William Street.

celebrity chef

noun, 1. (male) person who swears a lot in the kitchen. **2.** (female) person who eats as if she were giving a blowjob

It used to be that celebrity chefs were the people who cooked meals for celebrities. Now it is the chefs who are celebrities. Go figure.

---

[1] Okay, so only I remember where I was.

challenge

noun, 1. problem

Bastards do not have problems, only challenges. Furthermore, they claim to 'enjoy a challenge', which is like saying they love having problems. Of course, they do not enjoy challenges at all, any more than they are **team players** or **people persons**, but they have a formless feeling that it would be a good thing if they did.

If they really liked a challenge, they could try telling the truth for a day — or just for a meeting. They could attempt to give a speech without using a sporting analogy, or read a book that did not come from the self-help shelves. They could even shut up and listen to other people for a change.

chardonnay

noun, 1. extremely common, cheap white wine, often drunk by Howard's battlers, or 'chardonnay conservatives'

Through no fault of its own, the innocent bottle of chardonnay — like the previously apolitical café latte — became a jagged-edged weapon in the long struggle by people on the right to annoy people on the left by claiming they prefer expensive drinks. For many blurry years, the podgy, grape-faced, brown-toothed, conservative dementariat referred to the 'middle-class left' as 'champagne socialists', until it became apparent that nobody outside their own circles drank champagne very much, except at weddings.

'Champagne socialists' gave way to 'chardonnay socialists' because chardonnay, while cheaper than champagne, cost more than the long-vanished long-necks of Dinner Ale that the dementariat imagined adorned the bare wood tables in battlers' cottages in industrial suburbs they never had occasion to visit.

Today, chardonnay is the most widely grown grape in Australia. The wine has acquired its own affectionate diminutive, 'shardy', and is found at barbecues throughout the battler belt and the bush. It is cheaper to get drunk on chardonnay than beer, and four- or five-litre casks are often the drink of choice among the **elite** who sleep on the streets and shout, 'Aaaaaargh, ya fucken… ya fucken… aaaaaaaargh!' at passers-by.

Meanwhile, the middle-class are said to prefer ABC ('Anything But Chardonnay'). As a result, the dementariat, waving the wrong end of the stick as if it were a flagpole, goes hunting for socialists at our national broadcaster.

Late-breaking news: due to EU regulations, by the year 2009 it will be illegal to refer to anybody who is not a native-born member of the Socialist Party of France as either a 'champagne' or 'chardonnay' socialist.

charity collectors, smiling, waving, jumping-into-your-path type of

noun, **1.** as above

A man once stopped me on Glebe Point Road, Sydney, and asked if I cared about the environment. I said, 'No,' because I don't. But that wasn't what he really wanted to know, anyway. He wanted to sell me a print of a drawing, and some of the money I gave to him, he would give to Greenpeace. Several other young men and women in the same spot were selling the same pictures.

Now, I like Greenpeace. I think it is great that the Green movement has a military wing that maintains its own navy and, like all great naval powers, has been to war with France, but I did not want to buy the drawing because it was crap.

The drawing sellers are long gone, and when I walk through the city today, I find myself nostalgic for simpler times. I miss the days when koala people owned the pavements and cycle couriers commanded the roads.

The koala people were the charity-collecting elite: volunteers who dressed in full-body koala bear-suits at the melting height of summer, fund-raising for the Wilderness Society.

'One of the meanest things we ever did was have them working on the streets of Cairns,' said Wilderness Society national director Alec Marr when I spoke to him recently. He seemed a bit suspicious as to why I should be asking about the extinct bears. 'They were on the point of death, so we had to keep them below the tropic of Capricorn,' he said.

At first, the koala people were relatively restrained, and simply stood around like marsupial *Big Issue* sellers who had mistakenly picked up a bucket. Gradually, they began a series of stunts to attract attention, ranging from lying on the pavement with their arms outstretched, to performing star jumps.

I had assumed there were hundreds — if not thousands — of them, but Alec assured me there were, at most, ten to 15 at any one point, and they were all the same people, travelling around the country.

Their suits were handmade by volunteers: 'They weren't consistent, if you know what I mean,' said Alec. Rumours quickly spread that some of the koala people were not actually Wilderness Society collectors, just people who had hired, bought or stolen their own koala suits. Alec said he only heard of this happening once, although it was a difficult situation to police, since only an expert could tell one koala from another. Perhaps in response to this, some koala people started to wear their big, droopy heads around their waists.

Some time in the new millennium, the koala person became extinct.

The koala person's natural habitat, the pavement, has been colonised by species more suited to urban life, such as vast colonies of sleepy-eyed T-shirt-wearing Amnesty International collectors, who are less prone to overheating.

I like Amnesty more than I like Greenpeace. I even signed up once, when it looked like the organisation was going to bring the murderous Chilean former-dictator Augusto Pinochet to justice. But I don't know any other members, so I was surprised when they started smiling at me in the street, and waving to me, and jumping in my path.

The new, hyper-cheerful Amnesty canvassers did not believe me when I said I was already a member and, eventually, they were right. I let my membership lapse when the UK foreign secretary Jack 'Man of' Straw allowed Augusto to be released from his luxurious house arrest in London, on the grounds that Jack, who is tough on all crimes except mass murder, would not know justice if it jumped out at him in the street wearing a koala suit, and had forgotten why he had become involved with politics in the first place.[1]

As pretending-to-know-you-already and acting-as-if-they-had-something-urgent-to-say-to-you became their chief tactics, street charity collectors became bastards for the first time (unless you count the counterfeit koala people). Like couriers, however, these things come in cycles. At time of writing, not only are there hardly any cycle couriers on the roads (or, more accurately, the pavements) but the canvassers have adopted a new spirit of restraint, and can now be treated with the same selective blindness you might employ as you pass a *Big Issue* seller, a homeless beggar, or **Alexander Downer** on fire outside a urinal.

cheese

noun, **1.** preferred diet of surrender monkeys

---

[1] The young Jack was active in Chile solidarity campaigns.

Anyone who does not appreciate God's gift of cheese is either (a) lactose intolerant; (b) a lunatic; or (c) my brother. But cheese, like chardonnay, unexpectedly found itself drafted to the front line of the fondly imagined 'culture wars' when US conservative commentator Jonah Goldberg used the phrase 'cheese-eating surrender monkeys' to describe the French. (Jonah had borrowed his words from an episode of *The Simpsons*.)

Recently, the phrase gained a wider coinage in Australia, chiefly among that curious sub-branch of the dementariat who append their own commentary to professional blogs, and write furious letters to broadsheet newspapers about subjects that anger them but do not affect them. 'Cheese-eating surrender monkeys' became an epithet for any person or nation that, on balance, did not believe that war brings peace.

This was before it became apparent that the US was about to begin a long and bloody process of surrender in Iraq, and cheese became the everyday dish of the day in the White House, Downing Street, Kirribilli House and whatever they call the official residence of the premier of Poland.

choice

noun. 1. (pertaining to work etc) no choice

Most people don't like choices any more than they like **challenges**. Most politicians, on the other hand, are fond of them. This is because most politicians have a much broader range of choices than most people. The choices that appeal to most people are between two good things: a red lolly and an orange lolly, for instance, or a Porsche and a Mercedes. Nobody is hanging out for a green lolly or a punch in the face to be added to the spread.

When given the choice, most people say they want government-funded schools and hospitals where education and health care are as good as anything the private sector can offer.

But this is not what politicians mean by choice. If people were choosing between two similar things, they would pick the one that did not directly cost them money, which is against the vibe of the thing. Therefore, the government funds okay schools, and subsidises the private sector to build better ones with the taxes paid by people who send their children to public schools. (In 1999, the filthy muck-raking Marxist terrorist Islamic unAustralian rag *The Economist* revealed that Rupert Murdoch had paid no net corporation tax in the UK for the previous 11 years. His profits during that period, the magazine estimated communistically, could have funded seven new hospitals, 50 secondary schools or 300 primary schools. In 2006, Rupert Murdoch was referred to as a 'Great Australian' by Liberal treasurer Peter 'Lou' Costello — the man in charge of collecting and distributing our tax revenue — nineteen years after Rupert had surrendered his Australian passport to become a citizen of the US.)

Other not-very-good choices include that offered to the people of Iraq by the Coalition Provisional Authority's James Haveman, the homosexually named Michigan social worker who was appointed to manage the post-war rehabilitation of the Iraqi health care system. Although free health-care was universal under the vicious tyrant Saddam Hussein — probably to maintain a fresh supply of healthy babies for the dictator to eat — James thought it best to introduce a fee every time Iraqis consulted a doctor, so as to instil in them a sense of personal responsibility and an understanding of the workings of the free market. Their choice was to pay for healthcare or remain ill.

The only people who want a choice between public and private health care, or public and private schools, are those who choose private. Un-coincidentally, those people are often politicians, or the **property developers** who fund them. No government minister ever sucked the sticky plastic wrapping off a green lolly. Politicians want rich people to have the choice to choose something better than everybody else, because otherwise there would be no point in being rich, and nobody would gather huge fortunes and pay no taxes on them, which is of great benefit to the economy.

Other choices that most people are not much interested in include WorkChoices, which may, in the lifetime of this book, bring down the Liberal government and introduce a Labor government that does the same things. Under WorkChoices, workers can choose to bargain away a lifetime of weekend penalty rates in exchange for something of equal value, such as a matchbox, a piece of string, or anything from the $2 shop. Even those rugged individualists for whom trade-union representation is the slimiest and snottiest of pre-licked green lollies do not want the choice of replacing it with no representation at all.

Few workers relish the idea of approaching their immediate bosses and big-noting themselves, only to be told that: (a) there is only a certain amount of money to go around, and if they get a pay-rise somebody else has to do without (during this discussion, the manager will continually refer to company funds as 'my money'); or (b) the manager would love to help, but it is really not his decision, and the **CEO** — who could not possibly find the time to meet everybody who feels they deserve a bigger slice of his cake — has vetoed the idea **at this juncture**.

cigarette

noun, **1.** a drug that is legal but nonetheless banned from every place you might want to use it, eg restaurants, bars, public transport, forecourts of petrol stations etc

My granddad stopped smoking at 60 years of age. He was about 75 when I asked him if he missed it.

'What do *you* think?' he replied, with uncharacteristic venom.

I have not smoked for ten years (give or take a couple of holiday binges) but I remember clearly the first cigarette of the morning, gratefully smoked in bed, with gluey eyes half-open and clogged lungs blocked shut. This was the best cigarette, with all the head-spinning power of a bucket bong.

It was chased closely by the second (and second-best) cigarette, smoked as a side dish at breakfast. Some things in life were meant to be together — Jagger and Richards, Lenin and Trotsky, hot chips and tomato sauce, me and Angelina Jolie — and foremost among them is a mug of tea and a fag.

The next best cigarettes were reward cigarettes, earned through some magnificent effort of will, such as reaching the top of a small hill (always difficult if you're a smoker) or eating a moderately filling meal.

Then came drinking cigarettes, taken to dry out the throat in preparation for further wetting of the whistle.[1] They were followed — as inevitably as day follows night and stalkers follow the newly famous — by hangover cigarettes, which made bearable, if only briefly, endless mornings scorched by headaches, inexplicable penury and amnesiac guilt.

When smoking was first banned from offices, and smokers still huddled in little groups outside every building, a cigarette was a passport to an exclusive club of people who (a) did about an hour's less work than everybody else; and (b) smelt funny. How we laughed at the silly non-smokers, who were expected to be always at their desks, even on sunny days. How we pitied our close cousins, the alcoholics, who, for some reason, were not allowed to pop out for five minutes every hour to get a drink.[2]

Restrictions engendered a new camaraderie among those smokers hardy enough to stand up to wowsers, managers, and colleagues who did not want to die from passive smoking. We were going to kill ourselves slowly, and do it on the boss's time.

---

[1] A little understood part of the human anatomy, found only in drinkers, believed to be located behind the tonsils.

[2] Although this is not strictly true of newspaper offices.

But cigarettes are bastards and liars and little white frauds. Long before I was old enough to drink, my family used to say I was born four drinks under par. The implication was I would only reach ordinary human levels of contentment after an hour and a half in the pub. Since my mum was a nurse, this proved to be a medically exact diagnosis. But nobody was ever born four cigarettes under par, because nobody who has never had a cigarette has ever needed one.

A glass of beer soothes, relaxes and allows you to forget your cares. (Ten glasses allow you to forget your address, and 15 to forget that there is a law against having sex with turtles.)

A cigarette, like an HR manager, does nothing useful. Its only function is to kill the desire for another cigarette, and the only reason you want another cigarette is that you smoked the last one. Nicotine provides blessed relief from nicotine starvation, and that is it. Sure, cigarettes calm you down, but you were only nervy and agitated because you were addicted to cigarettes in the first place.

My granddad died of lung cancer. Years later, I finally gave up smoking. It was the most difficult thing I have ever done, apart from the time I tried to put together my baby son's travelling cot.

I have friends who still smoke, and I am occasionally troubled by a feeling that I have betrayed them. I sometimes find myself jealously watching them kiss their cigarettes, as if they were lovers who left me.

I never actually crave cigarettes, but do I miss them?

Only when I breathe.

classical music

noun, 1. widely unpopular, heavily subsidised art form

Classical music does not attract many new composers, because to write good classical music you have to be dead. And yet, classical music was the pop music of its day, and performers such as Verdi, Schubert and Liszt were the hip-hop superstars of their era. In the Middle Ages, Chopin (pronounced 'shopping') was as controversial as Eminem; Beethoven was considered as sexy as Britney; and JS Bach, like rapper 50 Cent, was shot nine times while dealing crack to his homeboys.

columnist, fright-wing

noun, 1. liar

Liberal newspapers often employ columnists whose professed views are far to the right of the paper's own editorial, the opinions of its readers, and Pauline Hanson. Their chief preoccupations are usually political correctness and the undeserving poor. They are — or pretend to be — very angry that some people somewhere are getting something for nothing, particularly if they are recent arrivals to Australia, such as refugees or Aboriginals.

Fright-wing columnists are also concerned about rising crime, particularly when crime is not rising. They seem to want to scare their readers into thinking that Australia is a dangerous place, and that most of those dangers are posed by people from other cultures, whom they are not allowed to identify as criminals. One fright-wing columnist specialises in writing about how he is not allowed to write about the fact that some Lebanese people are criminals.

The fright-wingers portray themselves as the voices of the voiceless, the spokespeople of the marginalised majority. Week after dreary week, on the page opposite the editorial in the liberal media, they are given the space to complain that they are silenced by the liberal media, and never given the space to say so. They feel persecuted by the 'political correctness police', who are the only police they do not like.

Why are they given a platform? There are four reasons: (1) the readers like to dislike them; (2) the CEOs of the liberal newspapers secretly agree with them; (3) they provide a spurious balance to the editorials; (4) they stimulate mail.

I will tackle these points individually, like a grown-up writer:

(1) If readers did not write in, week after dreary week, complaining about the columnists, the papers' editors would decide that nobody read them, and they would be dropped. The columnists often get the most mail when they engage in humourless leftie-baiting, taking the so-called 'baby boomers' to task for their supposed fecklessness and promiscuity, and blaming all the social problems of the new millennium on the all-but-forgotten permissive society. Like BDSM sex and boxing, humourless-leftie-baiting is cruel but fun. If I were not a

humorous leftie, I would probably do it myself. Since there is ample evidence that the humourless leftie actually enjoys his baiting, it is a win–win situation.

As we have seen, left-wingers are regularly accused of chardonnay drinking, latte sipping, and also — most curious of all — basket-weaving. (The epithet 'basket weaver' was popularised by Labor prime minister Paul Keating, to describe people who lived in Balmain, which has the highest number of pubs of any Sydney suburb. 'Drunks' might be a more appropriate appellation, but drunkenness carries no opprobrium in the ALP, although basket-weaving has the mark of infamy.) If the humourless leftie refused to be baited, the fright-wing columnist would quickly die out.

There is a chance that they will disappear anyway, since the humourless leftie, once endemic, is now an endangered species. Due to changes in the socio-political landscape, many who would otherwise have become humourless lefties have opted instead to embrace humourless environmentalism, humourless new-age beliefs, or humourless motivational thinking. To stay on the left these days, you have to maintain a sense of humour, since things have not been going our way for a long, long time.

(2) CEOs like the fright-wing columnists because they inject a bit of common sense into the debate. CEOs get agitated when the Left suggests that the financial problems of the poor can be solved by giving them money, because they sense it is their money that is being talked about. They prefer creative fright-wing solutions, such as making them work for the dole, or locking them up.

(3) CEOs can become restive when the editorials in their own newspapers are not adequately supportive of rich people. They begin to sense a sinister conspiracy against them, perpetuated by journalists. Publishers and CEOs do not really like journalists or — if they come from a background in, for instance, the fast-food industry — they do not know any. They do not understand why it takes so many highly paid people to produce a newspaper, when you can run a branch of McDonald's with a dozen teenage counter staff and a Down's syndrome boy to mop the floors. You cannot rely on journalists to make these points in the newspaper, but an adequately paid fright-wing columnist will bang on about the debilitating effects of trade-union power long after the trade unions have ceased to have any power.

(4) Ninety per cent of readers who write in to newspapers are mad. This probably has less to do with the proportion of mentally ill people among the readership of any given publication than with the amount of free time with which the mentally ill find themselves. The remaining ten per cent of readers are very angry. Even in these days of email, it takes immense provocation to move a sane person with a job and a family to send a letter to somebody they do not know about a third party they will never meet.

Many fright-wing columnists have ceased to be journalists in any meaningful sense. Nor do they seem to get their news from the papers they write for, preferring instead to gauge the mood of the nation from talkback radio grabs and government press releases. They are, traditionally, exorbitantly paid, which makes fright-wing scare-mongering a shrewd career move. Not many journalists are prepared to do it, so it is a seller's market. These factors combine to make the columnists unpopular with their colleagues. But when reasonable people meet a fright-wing columnist, they are often astonished how urbane and sophisticated the fright-winger can be. He is not a pork-skinned **taxi driver** with an exploding head. He is an erudite, educated, chardonnay-drinking, latte-sipping, cheese-eating, soon-to-announce-surrender-in-Iraq monkey. He does not believe all asylum seekers are criminals, any more than David Irving believes there were no gas chambers in the concentration camps. He just thinks that most people are stupid.

Most fright-wing columnists are laughably middle-class. In order to display their preternatural empathy with 'battlers', they are forced intellectually to embrace the **hate-radio** jocks, but it is an uncomfortable coupling. When they kiss, they do not tongue. All but the most stupid fright-wingers crinkle their noses at the whiff of another kind of gas in the windbags' wind.

comfort zone

noun, **1.** one of many imaginary places a bastard does not want to be, along with outside **the loop** and in the same room as an **invisible elephant**

conspiracy theory

***noun*, 1.** complex, disjointed and unfeasible explanation of disquieting events, favoured by idiots and often popularised by bastards for their own ends. **2.** shit film by Mel Gibson, a conspiracy theorist

Idiots love conspiracy theories, because they offer explanations as to why idiots are not more prominent in fields largely populated by bastards. They like to feel they are held back in life by Jews, Freemasons, homosexuals, the Illuminati or Opus Dei, rather than the fact that they are stupid.

Many conspiracy theories originate in their author's conviction that things did not happen: the moon landing, the Holocaust or the September 11 attacks, for instance.

If you are a **media sceptic**, or just an idiot, you can gather 'evidence' that anything did not happen. I once read a piece in *Lock Stock & Barrel*, a defunct right-wing magazine published in Queensland, that asked how it was that North Vietnam was supposed to have been heavily bombed by the US when anybody could see there are still loads of buildings in Hanoi. I myself do not believe there is a country called Kyrgyzstan.

Among the world's most prominent conspiracy-theorising political movements is Hamas, the democratically elected government of the Palestinian people, who voted for them even though they do not agree with them (for further information on the curious relationship between Muslims — and Jews — and their leaders, see **Sheik Taj Din al-Hilali** and **War on Terror**). Three articles in Hamas's constitution (or Covenant) expose Freemasons, Rotary Clubs and Lions Clubs as 'nothing more than cells of subversion and saboteurs' working in the interests of Zionism, which is 'behind the drug trade and alcoholism in all its kinds'.

Other conspiracy theories are built on the premise that lone gunmen did not act alone. Many people — most of them Queenslanders — believe mad Martin Bryant's Port Arthur murder spree was orchestrated by the state, to give it an excuse to strip gun owners of their weapons and leave them defenceless against the New World Order's push to subjugate the population through fluoridisation of the water supply.

Bastards often perpetuate conspiracy theories even when they do not actually believe them, especially when it helps to further their political ambitions. There is no need to give an obvious historical example here. Let's just say that David Irving says it did not happen.

Some idiots believe that the moon landing was faked. One of them, Bart Sibrel, approached astronaut Buzz Aldrin, the second man to walk on the moon, and demanded he swear on the Bible that he actually went there. Buzz punched him in the face.

This is a reasonable reply to most conspiracy theorists.

consultant

noun, **1.** person whose expertise lies in the field of self-promotion. **2.** the last person a rational being would consult about anything. **3.** sanitary napkin. Eg 'She's got the consultants in'

When a manager on the inside does not know what to do, he calls in a consultant, who is somebody from the outside who does not know what to do. This is despite the fact managers are paid large amounts of money to know what to do. The manager might argue he is displaying the depth of his knowledge by knowing when to delegate, but if you believe that then you believe flavoured milk comes from **purple cows**.

A consultant is somebody who was fired from his last job under cover of resignation or a move 'sideways' into 'special projects'. He has set up on his own because no other firm will hire him on his previous salary, and he believes it will exempt him from paying tax.

His office is a desk in his bedroom. The assistant's voice on his answering machine belongs to his wife or daughter. His largest capital investment is his fancy business cards, and there is nothing in his briefcase but sandwiches.

Before he arrives — and even up to two weeks into his tenure — he will be hailed as a genius, a guru, the man who will turn the situation around etc. You will be very lucky to have him, as he spends most of the year in the US.

Consultants deliver the same speeches wherever they go, prescribe the same solutions no matter what the problems, and hold workshops that bewilder and anger the staff who are forced to participate. They write reports addressing the issues on which they have been consulted, and these are ignored. The consultant is then systematically vilified, his presence is blamed on somebody who has since left the company, and within months the very fact he was once hired has been forgotten.

At the point where corporate amnesia is complete, another consultant is hired.

consultant, building industry

noun, **1.** crook

consultant, industrial relations

noun, **1.** standover man

consultant, industrial relations (building industry)

noun, **1.** hitman

corporate warriors

CEO *noun*, **1.** Consumingly Egotistical Oddity. **CFO** *noun*, **1.** Clerically Fixated Obstacle. **CIO** *noun*, **1.** Clothing Indifferent Outsider. **2.** fat geek. **C-3PO** *noun*, **1.** absurd robot carefully programmed to be loyal to its masters

The militarisation of corporate titles is either the first step towards a national managerial dictatorship, or another symptom of the comical arrogance of managers who, through decades of hagiographic business journalism, have come to think of themselves as corporate warriors.

The use of the terms 'chief' and 'officer' to describe the private schoolboy sitting at the head of the board table in a Zegna suit and women's underwear, is supposed to lend him the air of a leader of men. He is more likely to be an unprincipled careerist with no sense of shame, who would sacrifice his company for personal gain. In this, at least, he is similar to military commanders throughout history.

In the corporate army, the CEO has other C-O types who — in a suitably military manner — 'report' to him. These include the CFO, a shabby, uninteresting fellow who wears a slightly worse suit than the boss and may harbour ambitions to become the COO, or Crushingly Ordinary Oligarch.[1] (This is like a CEO but without the minuscule charisma that more flamboyant executives can bring to the role.)

---

[1] None of the above applies to my mate Chris, as brave and noble a CFO as ever led a team of fearless accountants into battle. Chris would never ask his men to do anything he would not do himself, and would always be the first over the top at a dangerous audit.

CFOs (who are really just accountants wearing signet rings) are multiplying (asexually, of course) faster than even arithmetically obsessed CFOs can multiply, and even the smallest company has one of these brave soldiers on its general staff. Eventually, we will know exactly how many beans there are in the world, and then they will have to start counting them again.

The saddest C-O of them all is the CIO, who never wanted to join the army. He does not like to wear a suit, which he considers a primitive pretension of advanced, bipedal, carbon-based life-forms, so he buys the cheapest model and offsets any lingering sartorial effect with a cartoon tie. He would prefer to come to work dressed as Dr Who and, ideally, he would take the title 'Time Lord'.

He is uncomfortable with his fellow officers. He suspects the CEO would have beaten him up at school, and the CFO would have beaten him in maths tests. Although he is the least military minded of all the C-Os, he is the one most likely to turn up to work with a firearm and shoot everybody.

Most junior executives and assistant managers could be described as C-3POs, because they (a) robotically adhere to their masters' wishes; (b) fear action; and (c) regard themselves primarily as communicators.

Business culture reached the height of its macho pretensions in the 1980s–1990s, when it became fashionable for executives to read Sun Tzu's *The Art of War* and, more surreally still, Carl Von Clausewitz's *On War*. Sun Tzu assured them that 'The Commander stands for the virtues of wisdom, sincerity, benevolence, courage and strictness.' Von Clausewitz taught them the defence of swamps, and the attack of morasses, inundations and woods. Imbued with a new military confidence, businesspeople began to take on names that would strike fear into the hearts of the enemy (ie workers).

The most famous of these to wash his bloody boots in an Australian boardroom was 'Chainsaw Al' Dunlap, the 'Rambo in Pinstripes'. His real name was Albert Dunlap, but 'Chainsaw Albert' sounds more like a character in *Bob the Builder* than a ruthless corporate downsizer. Chainsaw Albert went into companies, closed down departments, sacked employees and increased the value of the companies' shares by doing so. That was the theory, but Albert the Chainsaw ('Can he cut it? Yes he can!') — who had attended West Point Military College and therefore *really was an officer* (sort of) — turned out to be a mean-minded fraud who could not actually build a company if you gave him a stockpile of pink plastic bricks and a whole gang of ethnically diverse animatronic helpmates.

In Australia, Albert the Chainsaw was hired by Kerry Packer to cut the dead wood from his companies. He succeeded in driving out executives who immediately went on to found OzEmail, a company that would arguably have made more profit for Kerry than anything he lost on the various peripherals he shed.

In 1998, Albert the Chainsaw was downsized from his job as CEO at the Sunbeam-Oyster corporation and was later forced to pay shareholders $15 million to settle a lawsuit against him. He also copped a $500,000 fine and was banned from holding office in a public company again. Sunbeam-Oyster went into bankruptcy three years later.

countries, new

***noun,* 1.** countries, old, bits of

There are a couple of different theories as to where the Dapins come from. Darwinians believe we descended from monkeys — specifically, proboscis monkeys — but I like to think we are a cross between humans and beer.

It's hard to be certain, because there are so few of us around. For a long time, the Dapins thought 'Dapin' was a made-up word, invented by British customs officers who could not spell 'Dapzhenitsyn' or 'Dapinstoyevsky' or whatever my Russian great-grandparents volunteered as their name.

We small but disgruntled band of British Dapins — numbering less than 20 in three generations — were the only family we knew. The others, we guessed, had been wiped out in pogroms, the Holocaust, or the Great Patriotic War. Then, one day, I got an email from somebody who was trying to register 'mdapin' as part of her own email address, and found it already taken. She asked if I was a relative, and it turned out I probably was. Her ancestors, like mine, had fled their burning villages in the dying years of the 19th century, their neighbours slaughtered by peasants urged on by priests, police and Alandropov Jonesevik.

While the British Dapins became cabinet makers, the American Dapins went west and set themselves up as fur traders. There is a Dapin Road in Madison, Wisconsin, along which cowboy Dapins once strode with bow-legged pride, their six-guns at their hips, their Stetsons set at a jaunty angle, and their fob-watches positioned over their hearts to protect them from the treacherous bullets of their mortal enemies, the ornery, no-good, double-crossing **Downer**s.

The US Dapins have discovered our ancestors lived in Belarus, which was an independent nation for a couple of years from 1918, then a Soviet republic until 1990, and now seems on the verge of becoming the first former Soviet republic to return to the Russian Federation. This is a good thing. There was no need for Belarus to reappear. Terrible things happened to innocent Dapins there.

In fact, the post-Soviet world is home to a number of new countries with no useful function. Most of them are at least semi-tyrannies (the exception being Kyrgyzstan, which does not actually exist). Turkmenistan, until recently, was a dictatorship run by the late President for Life Saparmurat Niyazov, who renamed the days of the week after members of his family, and changed the word for 'bread' to the name of his mother. Even the 'Leader of all Turkmen' has some progressive policies, however: in 2001, he banned young men from wearing **beard**s.

When a great empire crumbles, it inevitably leaves behind hollow geographical anomalies that exist just to annoy their neighbours (look at New Zealand, for example). The emergence of new nations isn't always a bad thing. The anti-colonial struggles after the Great Patriotic War led to the birth of the world's tiny-but-sorely-needed stock of nations beginning with 'Z': Zambia and Zimbabwe. On the other hand, there is obviously an element of duplication in having one country called Niger and another called Nigeria, especially when they are next to each other.

While I remain true to the faith of my fathers — a world socialist state, without poverty, racism, war or 'marketing gurus'[1] — I don't understand what anti-globalisation protestors have against globalising. Would they prefer a return to the villainous Mercator projection, by which tiny, insignificant countries such as the USA were made to seem larger than vast African superpowers such as Niger?

We need fewer countries on the planet, with fewer borders, fewer nationalists, fewer despots and fewer beards. Only then will Dapins feel safe to sit around drinking beer and putting the world to rights.

For a list of imaginary countries that should exist in preference to Belarus, see **Appendix B: A List of Imaginary Countries that Should Exist in Preference to Belarus**.

COW

noun, **1.** a ruminant mammal, supposedly

They are planning something. Mark my words.

---

[1] This is not to suggest belief in a world socialist state was the faith of my actual father, who was a pragmatic man, more deeply concerned with the fortunes of Liverpool Football Club.

creationist

noun, 1. idiot

Creationists believe God created the world in six days, and Adam and Eve lived in the Garden of Eden until Eve was persuaded by a snake to eat an apple, whereupon the First Couple were packed off to this vale of tears.

The problem with this story is that in modern times snakes do not have the power of speech. People who scoff at the idea of evolution, and think it ridiculous that monkeys might have grown into men, nonetheless accept that reptiles have gone through a kind of reverse evolutionary transformation from intelligent, loquacious, seductive beings, into the mute, repulsive coils of mouse-eating garden hose they are today.

creative

noun, 1. word used by non-creative people to describe something they copied from somewhere else. 2. word used by non-creative people to describe themselves

A creative is a person at an advertising agency who is responsible for *the* creative. *The* creative is that part of the advertisement they have stolen from a popular movie, TV show, song or long-running page in *Viz* comics.

In the advertising industry, 'creative' is a comparative term. The copywriter probably is more creative than the account executives, but less creative than, for example, a tree. To elaborate, I was recently taking my country-town breakfast at the local McDonald's (I know, I know) when I noticed a colourful flyer lining my tray. It alerted me to the fact that, contrary to rumour, pig fat was not used in the manufacturing of McDonald's soft serves. I had never heard anyone claim otherwise, but now I have.

It is part of a wider campaign that appears to have been designed by creatives for McDonald's to draw attention to the various charges against the fast-food giant. On the internet, I followed McDonald's weblink to http://makeupyourownmind.com.au, and discovered that the company does not use powdered eggs. I didn't even know powdered eggs existed. Nor does its Filet-o-Fish contain dolphin. I had never been told it might. I had heard some of the other accusations refuted by the website — that McDonald's cuts down rainforest timber, and its French fries are made from potatoes mixed with flour — but I had forgotten them. Until now.

Next door to McDonald's was — of course — a KFC outlet, but its management did not feel compelled to distribute a disclaimer that nobody had ever really bitten into a Kentucky fried rat. There were also three Chinese restaurants in town, but none prefaced their menu with a reminder that no dogs or cats were harmed in the making of their chop suey. This is because KFC does not even admit to selling fried chicken any more, and small-town Chinese restaurants cannot afford to hire creatives to bolster their reputations.

The government, however — if it has any funds left over after subsidising **Amanda Vanstone**'s education — can use taxpayers' money to sign up thousands of clever creatives to sell its curiously unpopular policy of robbing the poor to pay the rich. In August 2007, it paid creatives to persuade people to stop worrying about whether WorkChoices would mean they would lose their holiday entitlements, penalty rates etc. The creatives tackled this **challenge** by filming television advertisements showing ordinary people talking about how they were worried that WorkChoices would mean they would lose their holiday entitlements, penalty rates etc.

Unfortunately, most people who saw the ads agreed with the workers, and dismissed the Workplace Authority director's reassurances. The market-research company that studied the impact of the campaign said it was 'educating the public as to the negative realities of the new IR laws rather than myth-busting'.[1]

So who says creatives are the bad guys?

cricket

noun, **1.** a pestilence named after a pest

I have the utmost respect for our prime minister. He is firm but fair. He is tall, dark and handsome. He sends out **fridge magnets** to fight wars, instead of expensive and non-adhesive soldiers. But his most fantastic idea is undoubtedly the 'citizenship test', by which newcomers to this country would be

---

[1] 'Howard's New IR Ad Blitz Backfiring', *The Weekend Australian*, 4/8/07.

assessed on their basic understanding of our history and values. The former leader of the Opposition, Kim Beazley, suggested this be applied to tourists, too. The National Party, a minor agrarian-socialist cult, has proposed that immigrants be quizzed on the noble role of regional Australia, and John Howard has refused to rule out the inclusion of a question about cricket.

This is very clever indeed.

The birthplace of modern suicide terrorism is Sri Lanka, where cricket is the national sport. In Pakistan, the cradle of the Taliban, cricket is the national sport. One of the July 7 London bombers, Shehzad Tanweer, was a schoolboy cricketer. Another, Hasib Mir Hussain, played for his local cricket team in Leeds. Evidence has emerged that the bombers planned at first to attack the Australian and English teams at the Edgbaston Test, but called it off because they were cricket fans.

There is something about cricket that is fundamentally attractive to terrorists.

Perhaps it is the grotesque symbolism of 'the Ashes', which are surely intended to represent the ashes of Western civilisation. Maybe it is the maiden over, clearly a reference to one of the 72 virgins that suicide bombers expect to meet in heaven. Could it be the obvious resemblance between traditional cricket 'whites' and the all-white outfit modelled by the imbecilic Bali bomber, Amrozi, complete with 'cap'? It might simply be that, like a holy war, a cricket match goes on forever. More than likely, it is a combination of all these things.

It is vitally important that all potential immigrants are grilled to find out exactly how much they know about this sinister 'game'. Questions could include 'What exactly is silly mid off?'

and — if they get that one right — 'Why do you want to blow up the world?'

If swarthy foreigners can so much as identify Donald Bradman from a photofit picture, they should be bundled back onto their boat and sunk before they get the chance to throw their children overboard.

If in doubt, run them 'out'.

curry, available spiced according to your tastes

noun, **1.** chilli stew

I was outside an Indian restaurant in Queenstown, New Zealand, scanning the menu for the tell-tale sign that the establishment was actually a hollow sham, a shameful facsimile of a genuine curry house, and an insult to the memory of the great Indian cook, Madhur Jaffrey (who is not, in fact, dead).

This usually appears in italics at the foot of the menu, and runs along the lines of: 'Please tell your waiter if you require your meal mild, medium or hot.'

It is not possible to cook, for instance, a mild vindaloo. A vindaloo is hot by virtue of the combination of its ingredients, in the same way as bacalhau is salty, venison soup is gamey, and my own speciality, jacket potatoes and cheese, is potatoey and cheesy.

If the same 'curry' can be served mild, medium or hot, then the flavour can only come from the amount of chilli powder sprinkled into the sauce. It is not a curry at all, it is a sort of watery chilli broth.

There was no such rider on the menu, so we went inside. The tables were heavy with grey nomads, roaming the antipodes in search of the town with the cheapest pharmacist. This would usually sound a warning. As we grow older our palates change to accommodate our dentures and our reactionary political views, and we start to think of fush and chups as dangerously spicy.

Sure enough, when the waiter arrived, he made the 'mild, medium or hot' offer and, sure enough, when the curries arrived, they consisted of pre-cooked meat, reheated in a sad, pointless soup. Madhur Jaffrey would have turned in her grave (except she is not, in fact, dead).

I don't blame the Indian restaurateurs, who are only catering to the market. The real villains are the people who ask for mild curries in the first place. Here's a thought: if you don't like Indian food, why not get the fuck out of Indian restaurants and leave them to those of us who do?

Downer, Alexander

noun, **1.** a post-flatulent smirk. Eg 'Look at the Alexander Downer on that Cheshire cat. He must have farted'

Alexander Downer, the Foreign Mincer, seems to suffer from what might be called 'Downer's syndrome' — an inability to give a straight answer to a question.

Whenever he is interviewed, he wears a look on his face that says, 'I know your game, mate. You're trying to get me to own up to the bad smell. Well, you know I did it and I know I did, but we both know I'm never, ever going to dob myself in. So what're you gonna do about it? Eh?'

At this point, this remarkably eloquent expression leans out of the TV and prods you in the chest.

Of course, Downer's syndrome is so prevalent in Federal Parliament it is believed to be carried by bacteria that can only live in heavily subsidised food, and Alex was far from the most advanced sufferer. A particularly sad case of Downer's was the former Federal Minister for Workplace Relations, Kevin Andrews, who believed employees were holding bosses to ransom by demanding money in exchange for work. He never replied to an interviewer's query; he just said something at random. If you asked him his favourite colour, he would nominate 'Neil Armstrong'.

Breakfast at the Andrews house must be a surreal affair.

Mrs Andrews: How would you like your eggs, Kevin?

Big Kev: Somalia.

Mrs Andrews: Tea or coffee?

Big Kev: Lungfish.

But who is Alexander Downer, and is he really more down than Alexander Down, but less down than Alexander Downest? Alexander John Gosse Downer is a bloody-nosed battler from the wrong side of the tracks who, through sheer guts, determination and brains, fought his way to become a government minister in the Liberal Party. He was aided only slightly by the fact that his pater, also called Alexander Downer, was also a government minister in the Liberal Party.

Alex was educated at Geelong Grammar, a notoriously tough inner-city school dominated by the children of recent immigrants and housing-commission tenants. He braved further hardship when he attended university in the British city of Newcastle. He is now the Federal MP for Mayo, the sole condiment with a seat in parliament. This is believed to be part of the so-called 'Downer Gerrymander' which ensures there is always an Alexander Downer in parliament, even if his only constituency is salad cream.

He led the Liberal Party for eight months in 1994–5, during which the Liberal Party did nothing at all. Nonetheless, he always looks very pleased with himself about something. What makes him so complacent?

I asked Kevin Andrews.[1]

'The antechinus is a nocturnal marsupial,' he replied.

duck

noun, **1.** a member of the Anatidae family of mostly aquatic birds

Obviously, I've got nothing against ducks per se, although I do feel that, like **xylophones**, they are over-represented in children's literature. But bastards, like children, cannot get enough of ducks. They have recently added the disciplined duck to their imaginary menagerie of unnatural animals such as the **purple cow** and the **invisible elephant**.

When everything is working smoothly, **consultants** believe they have all their ducks in a line (or row). They feel that the linear arrangement of waterfowl symbolises a state of perfect organisation.

---

[1] I didn't really.

In fact, ducks need no prompting from management to swim in a row. It is instinctive behaviour.

Still, at least 'ducks in a row' is not another of the colourful North American sporting metaphors that make bastards' conversation so interesting and illuminating. Or is it?

Although an estimated 95 per cent[1] of bastards believe that, if it were not for their efforts, most ducks would be flapping around anarchically or travelling in concentric circles, the phrase actually originated in the exciting world of tenpin bowling. Small tenpins used to be called duckpins. Whoever had all of his in a row was ready to knock them down again. This is the reason why, as soon as management believes it has lined up its ducks, everything topples over.

---

[1] Author's estimate, based on a sample of zero.

eight ball, behind the

noun, **1.** a bad place to be. Eg North Sydney, **Liechtenstein**

When a bastard first told me 'we' were (ie he was) behind the eight ball 'on this one', I thought he meant he was well placed to score the winning shot. I could not understand why he seemed anxious, unless he was scheming to lose a game of pool to an attractive woman, in order to trick her into bed with him. Because every woman loves a man who loses at pool.

It took me several years to figure out that he actually felt he was behind the eight ball at an inappropriately early stage of the game — when he was aiming, for instance, to pot the two ball, the 11 ball or the 14 ball. He was, in fact, snookered.

In order to get out from behind the eight ball, you have to bounce the cue ball off the cushion. This is not such a difficult task, requiring only minimal hand-eye coordination, and it is time bastards became more relaxed about it.

elephant, invisible

noun, **1.** elephant, non-existent

Bastards believe that when nobody in a room will acknowledge an obvious fact, it is because they cannot see an elephant. The idea is that an elephant is so big, it blots out everything else. This is a rather juvenile conception of an elephant, based on a poor understanding of human spatial awareness. Although an elephant is, indeed, a large animal, even a small child could see both ends of it at once.

If the elephant in the room really was invisible — say, for example, its refractive index was altered to that of air — its presence would soon become obvious by the smell of its droppings, although this could easily be mistaken for the stench of marketing bullshit.

Bastard-busting tip number three: Keep a wad of psychiatrists' business cards in your wallet or handbag. When a bastard suggests there is an invisible elephant in the room, wordlessly hand them a card.

elite

***noun,* 1.** any person who is cleverer than you and does not agree with you

I was reading an article in a right-wing magazine in which the writer referred to his opponents as 'what might be described properly as the chattering classes', as if he had undertaken a rigorous taxonomic study of contemporary Australia, and separated the chattering classes from the nattering classes, the murmuring classes, the bellowing classes and so on. The writer was a member of what might be described properly as 'the dissembling classes', whose picture of the world is as incoherent as, for example, **Santo Santoro**'s declaration of his share tradings in the Senate Register.

Australian right-wingers love to characterise themselves as victims. There is a conspiracy against them, they pretend to believe, led by the elites. In fact, they suffer from a psychiatric problem known as anosognosia, or unawareness of their own condition. By elites, they do not mean people such as **Alexander Downer**, the private-school-educated multimillionaire politician son of a former Liberal politician called Alexander Downer; or **Philip** Maxwell **Ruddock**, the private-school-educated multimillionaire son of a former Liberal politician called Maxwell Ruddock; or even Miranda Devine, the private-school-educated journalist daughter of a former national newspaper editor called Frank Devine.

In fact, people such as Miranda, who lives on Sydney's North Shore and is married to a senior manager at Lend Lease, are most likely to point to people who do not have rich, influential parents as belonging to elites. David Flint, lawyer, academic and former head of the Australian Broadcasting Authority, wrote a book attacking the 'elite media' (surely not a wholly appropriate target for a broadcasting regulator), but David was leader of Australians for Constitutional Monarchy, an organisation supporting one of the richest and most powerful hereditary elites in the world, the German **royal family**.

When the right speak of elites, they do not mean hereditary elites — of which they are broadly in favour — or social elites, or financial elites. They mean teachers, university lecturers, ordinary working journalists and, um, social workers, who are against racism and in favour of universal social welfare.

They call them elites because they are clever, even though they sometimes did not even go to a private school. This, in the eyes of right-wingers and **fright-wingers**, is an appalling form of arrogance, and a deliberate attempt to put themselves above ordinary people, who right-wingers believe are irredeemably stupid.

I would love to live in the country the latte-sipping, chardonnay-drinking, cheese-eating, soon-to-announce-surrender-in-Iraq monkeys describe, where leftists control even the Murdoch press, and simple bigots are mercilessly brainwashed into believing in liberty, equality and fraternity by a sinister but all-powerful alliance of academics, historians, political commentators and home craftspeople such as basket weavers.

Instead, however, I live in a nation run by Alexander Downer, Philip Ruddock et al, where the Murdoch press is controlled by

Rupert Murdoch, and even basket-weaving is outsourced to sweat shops in Vietnam.

enlightenment

noun, **1.** protection racket for cows

The Indian subcontinent is a land teeming with filthy, squalid people, dressed in rags. These are called 'backpackers' and many of them are searching for enlightenment. India is famous for having loads of enlightenment. There is even an Enlightenment University in Pune, where you can get a degree in enlightenment.

Westerners often come to India to find themselves. Those who are successful presumably left themselves in India in the first place. The rest are more likely to find **cows**. There is almost as much stray cattle in India as there is enlightenment.

The roads of New Delhi are choked with grey, emaciated cows, living a hectic, inner-city lifestyle that must be quite bewildering for a ruminant. The cow, of course, is a miraculous animal, the source of both the beef patty *and* the slice of processed cheese in a hamburger, and the provider of the base ingredient for a wide range of flavoured milk drinks. I may have reservations about the beasts' plans for the future, and a particular suspicion of purple breeds, but Hindus believe the cow is sacred, as is their prerogative. However, the next person to find enlightenment might consider making rocket lettuce sacred instead, because (a) it tastes like poison; and (b) even if left entirely to its own devices, it would be unlikely to pose a major traffic hazard.

Not everybody can afford the time off work to go to India for 30 years and get enlightened. Luckily, many Australian organisations can offer a similar experience, although enlightenment in westerners tends to take a subtly different form to enlightenment in Indians. Whereas Indians searching for enlightenment might, for instance, take off all their clothes and climb a ladder of razors to the top of a 15-metre pole and stay there for six months eating nothing but the insects that fly into their mouths, westerners are more likely to sign up for two consecutive weekends of 'training' at the Landmark Forum.

Upon achieving enlightenment, they are unlikely to denounce the material world and go and live among lepers. Instead, they tend to start their own small businesses, often based around a fantastically banal ambition such as having always wanted to paint patterns on T-shirts, or sell organic watercress.

People whose busy lives prevent them from even putting aside four days to become enlightened can still find out about enlightenment from a quarterly magazine called *What Is Enlightenment?*. If you should need even more enlightenment than can be had from the pages of a glossy magazine, you can sign up for a Master's Degree program in Conscious Evolution. This is offered by *What Is Enlightenment?* in conjunction with the highly regarded Graduate Institute, which also runs MAs in Experiential Health and Healing, and Holistic Thinking.

When searching for enlightenment, it is important to have a guru. Gurus are often **beard**ed, and generally require female enlightenment-seekers to have sex with them. Men might prefer to simply give them all their money.

entrepreneur

noun, **1.** crook

estate agent

noun, **1.** crook

executive coach

noun, **1.** see **life coach**. **2.** crook

executive toy

noun, 1. fridge magnet for a desk

The 1980s saw many strange crazes — big hair, deely boppers, legwarmers, criminal Western Australian entrepreneurs — but the oddest was the fashion for adult managers to take toys to work. It was illuminating to note which toys seemed to appeal to executives. They were bright and shiny and mindlessly repetitious: little balls on strings that banged together, or two stick people on a seesaw that bounced up and down. If factory workers began decorating their workbenches with similar stuff, their supervisor would think they were retarded.

finance department

noun, 1. department found in large companies, responsible for losing invoices 'in the system'

While I was writing this book, it happened to me again. I almost could not believe it. I had just finished editing another semi-crazed, six-paragraph screed, demanding to know *what it is these people actually do*, and they did it to me again.

I had written a freelance story for a women's magazine (which shall remain anonymous, except to say that it has the same name as many French women), a month had gone by since I'd submitted my invoice, and I hadn't been paid. I had phoned the features editor, who said — as they always do, as I always did myself in similar positions — 'Well, you *should* have been paid,' as if I didn't know that. She checked with finance, and assured me the cheque would be in the post that day.

Maybe it was, but I didn't receive it. Another month passed, I wrote another story for the same magazine, the features editor emailed me to ask how it was coming along. I replied by asking how my initial payment was coming along.

She rang the finance department, and they were sorry but, once they had finally got around to processing my invoice, they had sent the cheque to the wrong address. It seems I had written something for another magazine in the same company two years before, and they had taken my details from that occasion. Rather than from my invoice.

Okay, so we all make mistakes. As any subeditor will attest, I make more than most. But they don't usually cost anybody anything. And I do not pride myself on my processes. Finance departments are founded on processes, and if my invoice does not conform to their standards, they do not pay it. Sometimes, they even tell me they are not going to pay it, but most of the time I have to ring up and ask. If I head the invoice 'invoice' instead of 'tax invoice', they won't pay it. If I miscalculate the total including GST, they can't change it for me and they won't pay it. If, however, I write my correct address on the invoice, they simply ignore it. They don't seem to have a process for checking if details have changed.

Suddenly, during my phone call with the features editor, my head exploded. I snapped that I did not need an apology from her, since it had nothing to do with her. I actually wanted to hear the finance person say sorry.

'Well, she's pretty high up…'

'High up in what?' I didn't say. She can't be high up in the scale of people on whom the magazine depends for its profits, because finance does not generate profits. The department simply takes a slab of revenue the magazine has earned through cover sales and advertising sales — both of which are dependent on the standard of writing and photography — and pays it to itself. In return for this, it distributes a share of the profits to the contributors whose work created those profits, and sends it to the wrong addresses.

That is assuming the invoice doesn't get 'lost in the system'. What does this actually mean? It means somebody deleted it, or threw it away.

I put down the phone, and demanded finance call me back.

A few minutes later, they did. They apologised, but couldn't promise they could pay me immediately, because *blah blah blah blah blah wooble-fish blah*.

How would they have felt, I wonder, if I had paid their salary to the wrong person, and could not immediately make good the mistake because *blah blah blah blah wooble-fish blah*.

Because the *real* bottom line — as distinct from finance's imaginary bottom line — is that we do pay their salaries. It would be refreshing if, now and then, somebody from finance acknowledged this.

The next week, I was not paid by my regular employer. The word from the finance department was that my invoice (like those of all the other 'vendors' that week) was 'inadvertantly (sic) left out while concatenating'. I assumed concatenating was a made-up word like 'inadvertantly', and meant 'the act of being unable to complete a simple book-keeping task because of the delusion one is turning into a concertina'. But it transpires it has a genuine Latin root and means to select or click on an entry. In other words, the finance department had not paid me because when they had received my invoice (and everybody else's) they had put it aside and forgotten about it. They might have thought it strange that nobody had invoiced that week, but they were probably all away on a **team-building** exercise.

financial planner

noun, **1.** crook

I first dipped a toe into the ocean of bastardry when my girlfriend at the time told me about her financial planner, whom she had visited for advice when she was $30,000 in debt. Rather than suggest she try to pay it all off as quickly as possible, he advised her to put some money aside for a savings plan.

This was a fantastically unproductive course of action, since every dollar she saved would be at the cost of the interest she would have to pay on every dollar she owed. Although her savings account also paid interest, she could not touch it for ten years. The financial planner received a commission for selling her the savings plan and, in those days, he did not have to declare it. And she defaulted after about a year anyway.

Her financial planner was planning his own finances using hers (and that was not all he was planning; he also lent her his

81

copy of *The Story of O*). Although financial planners are more tightly regulated now, and although their commission is supposed to come from the financial institutions rather than the 'client', they still take your girlfriend's money and use it to buy BDSM porn with which to seduce her.

flag

noun, **1. fridge magnet** for a stick

F-list celebrity

noun, **1.** 'Clayton's fame': the celebrity you have when you don't have celebrity

As the former editor of the men's magazine, *Ralph*, and the author of the worst-selling memoir, *Sex & Money*, I am no stranger to F-list celebrity. But life on the F-list isn't all two-free-beers-and-a-showbag — occasionally, you are called upon to give your expert opinion on things.

I was once invited to go on the radio and discuss why Mark Philippoussis had left Delta Goodrem for Paris Hilton. Not only had I never met any of these people, I'd never seen Mark Philippoussis play tennis, Delta Goodrem sing, or Paris Hilton do whatever it is she does — except on the internet, of course.

I declined, but my name continued to be linked with Paris Hilton.

I'm regularly asked to write about her, or even interview her, but there are only four questions anyone would want to put to Paris Hilton. (1) How did you feel when a private video tape of you having sex with your ex-boyfriend Rick Salomon allegedly entered the public domain? (2) How did you feel when a private video tape of you in the back of a car with your ex-boyfriend Nick Carter allegedly entered the public domain? (3) How did you feel when a private video tape of you naked with your ex-boyfriend Jason Shaw allegedly entered the public domain? (4) Are you starting to see any kind of a pattern here?

Recently, I was involved in a screen test for a new panel-style TV show. The cream of the F-list turned up at the studio: a cartoonist, a playwright, and a woman described to me as 'the maven of Aboriginal PR'.

I wasn't aware that Aboriginals had a PR — and if they have, it might be time to rethink their strategy, because they still suffer from a bit of an image problem.

Actually, the maven was very nice and sparkly and clever and articulate — as was everybody, except for me. We were given two topics to discuss. The first was the partial withdrawal of funding from state symphony orchestras, as recommended in a report by former Qantas CEO James Strong. In the time-honoured fashion of management consultants everywhere, Strong had suggested the orchestras would be more economical if they got rid of the musicians. He proposed, for instance, the Tasmanian Symphony Orchestra should lose nine of its 38 players. It wouldn't actually be able to play many symphonies any more, but what the heck.

I don't know anything about orchestras, so I went off about management consultants. Similarly, the maven championed Aboriginal music. The general feeling on the panel seemed to be that the government should fund underprivileged crews of indigenous rappers instead. Hmmm.

Our second subject was *The Da Vinci Code*, which only the playwright had looked at and nobody had read. I rambled about the Kabbalah, and the maven made some points about Aboriginal mysticism. I began to realise what an excellent PR she really was.

At the end, we each gave a short talk about something to do with culture. I chose Paris Hilton. I contended we did not see enough of her in magazines, in reality TV, in bookstores, or on the internet. Every appearance she makes is an argument against obscene privilege, private education and hereditary wealth. The sheer vacuous waste that characterises her life could see her become the Che Guevara of the trashbag generation — the image that inspires millions to rise up against the, er, giant hotel chains that oppress us all.

The only flaw in my case — which nobody was rude enough to point out — is the exact opposite has happened. Paris Hilton has, in fact, inspired millions of women and girls to dress and talk like her, and millions of boys and men to fantasise about her.

I'm not much of a pundit, and even less of a performer. Every time I spoke in the studio, I blushed. Even when I just produced that tragically eager, quickly truncated 'uergh' noise people make when they fail to break into a conversation, I felt myself turn tomato.

I didn't make the final cut for the show, but the whole casting process gave rise to fantasies of moving up from the F-list to the E-list — and maybe, one day, the D-list.

If I climbed high enough fast enough, I might even meet Paris Hilton on her way down. As it were.

For further information about how to achieve fame without fortune, see **Appendix C: How to be a Celebrity**.

focaccia

noun, **1.** salted packaging material

fridge magnet

noun, **1.** bastard

In the future, science fiction promised us robots, jet packs and cities in space. Instead, we got fridge magnets. Fridges, whose exterior surfaces were once vast canvases of plain white, as pure an artistic statement as anything Yves Klein produced, now look like pages torn from a mad philatelist's stamp album.

There is no aesthetic justification for fridge magnets. Most advertise the services of local tradespeople, but the day I look for a phone number on the fridge will be the day I store sausages in the *Yellow Pages*. They are what tools in **marketing** call 'marketing tools'. Tools used to be unimpeachable, in the days when they were things like saws and chisels, which could actually be used to make other stuff. These days, they can just as easily be advertisements or **PowerPoint presentations**.

Fridge magnets are ads that you stick up yourself, magnetic Mormons you invite into your home. They showed their true colours when they were co-opted into the so-called 'War on Laptops', in which governments continually come up with new ways to inconvenience people who want to take their computers onto planes, in case Osama bin Laden turns out to be hiding in Acrobat Reader.

In 2002, the year after al-Qaeda declared war on Australia by flying into the World Trade Center in Melbourne, the Howard government responded with a daring campaign of fridge magnets. They carried the fourth-form joke, 'Be alert, not alarmed', and the phone number for the national anti-terrorist hotline.

If a householder caught a glimpse of that familiar turbanned head at their kitchen window, they needed only look to the trusty Kelvinator for help and advice. One of those 'smart fridges' could probably dial the number itself.

The attorney general **Philip Ruddock** claimed the hotline received 50,000 calls in three years. Since considerably fewer than 100 suspected terrorists have been arrested, most of those calls must have been things like, 'There's a blockage in my cistern, please come at once. Ah, sorry, wrong fridge magnet.'

When the campaign was refreshed in 2005, the government decided to drop the fridge magnets. The nation had stood up as one and cried, 'If we have to resort to fridge magnets, the terrorists have already won.'

It made me proud to be Australian.

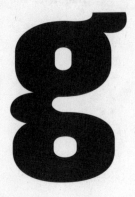

garden gnome

noun, 1. cheerful, bearded, fishing, plaster *Hitler*

Like the Bunsen burner, the refractive telescope and World War II, garden gnomes were a German idea, and their *volkish* bearing marks them as obviously anti-Semitic. Sympathisers claim to discern a deep, existential sorrow in the static lives of these **beard**ed ornaments, who are condemned forever to push an empty wheelbarrow up a hill, or fish futilely in an ornamental pond, but I see only malice and guilt.

In the last decade, the Garden Gnome Liberation Front was formed in France by misguided gnomanitarians. Some saw them as terrorists, others as freedom fighters, but nobody can deny that

GGLF guerrillas repeatedly and audaciously penetrated the heart of enemy territory, swooping on suburban gardens by night and stealing the furniture.

Under the auspices of the GGLF, 11 gnomes were hung by their necks under a bridge in eastern France. A nearby note said: 'By the time you read these few words, we will no longer be part of your selfish world, where we serve merely as pretty decoration.'

The organised pro-gnome movement has weathered blows, including the 1997 arrest and trial of five of its leaders for their part in the abduction of 150 gnomes. Politically, it was thought to be a spent force until the 'Strasbourg Incident' of 2001, in which about one hundred garden gnomes were found on a traffic roundabout, some arranged to spell the words 'Free the gnomes'.

Of course, gnomes are no more worthy of public sympathy than the defendants at the Nuremberg trials. To free them to go about their sinister business would be to unleash a plague of static, plaster, genocidal fanatics on the world outside our gardens. We are only safe so long as they are enclosed by topiary, fenced in with herbaceous borders, and overshadowed by tall, threatening trees.

Meanwhile, apolitical activists have long delighted in abducting gnomes, taking them overseas, and photographing them next to monuments such as the Leaning Tower of Pisa. It is too early to gauge what impact this 'stolen generation' of garden gnomes will have on the future of a race already decimated by the fact that no female garden gnome has ever been made, but I hope they die screaming with sharp things stuck in their heads.

golf

noun, **1.** a good walk ruined by Jews

Although not all professional golfers are bastards, recreational golf is the bastard's sport of choice. Many bastards love golf, and many more pretend to love golf, because playing golf is a good way of meeting fellow bastards and **networking**. There is little bastards enjoy more than getting together with a bag of dimpled balls, at an establishment that only recently began to admit Jewish people, and hitting them with clubs.[1]

Golf is a non-sport played by non-sportspeople. It is thought to have been founded in the Netherlands, which is suspicious in itself. The Chinese, who claim to have invented everything, reckon a similar game was played in 10th century China. If this is true, they had a 500-year start on the rest of the world, which explains why there are so many brilliant Chinese professional golfers around. They are thought to be outnumbered only by the Dutch.

Part of the appeal of golf is that each bastard has a caddy: a small, working-class person with amusing mannerisms who can be blamed when the bastard makes a mistake. Keen golfers include **elites**-bashing, hereditarily wealthy, private-school-educated, politician's son **Alexander Downer**, and Prime Minister John Howard. Chainsaw Al Dunlap lists golf as one of the hobbies he pursues in his retirement. **Santo Santoro**, the

---

[1] The balls, that is. It is no longer considered acceptable for bastards to hit Jewish people with clubs, no matter how 'pushy' they may find them.

former minister for amnesia, also liked to take time out from forgetting his share trades and criticising the lavish lifestyles of the industrial elite, to play a round of this most egalitarian of games.

gout

noun, **1.** disease of the toe, caused by not drinking enough alcohol. *proper noun,* **2.** unusual surname, shared by four people in the Sydney *White Pages,* all of whom probably swear it is pronounced 'goot'

I've always felt stalked by gout. I knew it would eventually catch up with me and stamp on my toe. It's the kind of humiliating illness to which I am prone. I already suffer from a thankfully mild case of gynaecomastea, unkindly known in bodybuilding circles as 'bitch's tit'. One of my nipples swelled up as if it were about to lactate, so I went to the doctor, who told me to stop taking steroids.

'But I've never taken steroids,' I protested.

'Give them up, then,' he said.

I also have world-class cholesterol. It was diagnosed by a communist doctor, who I enjoyed seeing because he addressed his patients as 'comrade'. When Comrade Doctor first tested me, I scored a level of 9.2. He showed me his cholesterol chart, which was calibrated from 0 to 8.

'This is about where you are,' he said, pointing to the space where New Zealand might be if the chart were a map of Australia.

I've been taking statins to bring my cholesterol down, but now I've got gout too.

It's surprising how little sympathy gout elicits from your friends (actually, it's not too surprising if you've already weathered the storms of laughter that greeted the announcement of your gynaecomastea).

I know you're bursting to tell me, 'Henry the Eighth had gout,' as if that's something nobody else knows.

Well, let me tell you, *everybody* else knows that.

'It's an old man's disease,' you say.

Is it really? I think you're confusing antiquity with old age. Henry the Eighth never even got to be an old man. He died at 56. So did my dad. And my dad had high cholesterol. Is that humorous enough for you?

I knew I had gout when my toe started throbbing as if it had been crushed under a horse's hoof. I went to my new, socialist doctor (the communist has gone to the outback to work with Aborigines), who did some tests and confirmed my self-diagnosis.

She told me gout is a build-up of uric acid in the joints. For some reason, the joint most often affected is the knuckle of the big toe, from which arise gout's rich comedic possibilities.

I'm fond of my doctor, but she can be quite predictable. She claimed people often developed gout from drinking too much.

'That's a fallacy,' I said, with the absolute confidence of the absolutely ignorant.

My doctor showed me the entry on gout in a fat, arrogant book called *General Practice* by Dr John Murtagh. It seemed broadly to support her crackpot theory.

I pointed out that anyone can buy themselves a PhD, and this Murtagh fellow probably downloaded his qualifications from the internet.[1]

She supported her argument with a 'fact sheet' (also from the internet) that listed among the condition's possible causes: too much beer, red wine or shellfish.

Shellfish. That would be it then. I ate a prawn cocktail in 1984. I've never actually had any shellfish since, which is just as well. I'd probably be dead by now. No wonder God warns against it in the Old Testament (Leviticus 11:10).

(Interestingly, doctors also finger shellfish — and alcohol — as cholesterol-raising factors, which points to a certain laxity in the medical profession when coming up with things to blame for stuff.)

The doctor prescribed anti-inflammatories, as usual, and told me, as usual, to drink less beer.

'Are there any diseases,' I asked, 'where you advise your patients to drink more beer and smoke cannabis?'

'Yes, there are,' she said. 'Fatal diseases.'

I bypassed the pharmacist, went straight to a party, drank ten schooners of Hoegaarden, and woke up with the usual throbbing, bulging, tender hangover — except this time it was in my toe.

---

[1] This book does not suggest that the eminent Australian physician Dr John Murtagh downloaded his qualifications from the internet, or that his standard GPs' text *General Practice* is arrogant or misleading. Although it is quite fat.

A humble voice in the back of my head whispered, 'Maybe you should give up drinking for a bit.'

'I'm sorry, humble voice,' I replied, in an exaggerated but unidentifiable foreign accent, 'I don't speaka de English.'

guru, marketing

noun, 1. marketing person who has paid a journalist to write a book for them

The most spine-chilling phrase in the corporate vocabulary is, 'I'd like you to meet our marketing guru.' The person who walks into the room will tell you nothing useful about anything, and he will do so with the aid of a **PowerPoint presentation**, an **invisible elephant**, and a vast catalogue of sporting metaphors, largely borrowed from baseball and gridiron.

A guru is a teacher in the Buddhist, Hindu and Sikh religions. A rabbi is the Jewish equivalent of a guru, and yet nobody is ever introduced as 'our marketing rabbi', even if they are Jewish. The concept of a marketing guru is racist. If you are forced into a meeting with one, you should complain to the Equal Opportunities Commission.

Bastard-busting tip number four: When a bastard is introduced to you as a guru (marketing, motivational or otherwise), throw yourself at his feet and ask him to interpret a particularly difficult passage from the *Maitrayaniya Upanishad*.

guru, motivational

noun, **1.** crook

habit

***noun,* 1.** (pertaining to people) rut, false comfort. **2.** (pertaining to bastards) bullshit

Bastards have been interested in habits since 1989, when the Latter Day Saint, Steven R. Covey, published *The Seven Habits of Highly Effective People.* While the saints of old — such as Peter and Paul — tended to write about religious matters, the newly-minted-in-Utah variety find themselves drawn towards management textbooks. 'Highly effective people' is American language for 'bastards'. Steven has many degrees, but he is no anthropologist. He has incorrectly identified many of the actual habits of bastards, and *Fridge Magnets are Bastards* could be seen as an academic correction of his earlier work.

Steven says habit one is 'be proactive'. Bastards are far more likely to 'be reactive'. They agree with everything their boss says, immediately, and when their boss contradicts himself, they react by agreeing just as quickly with his new opinion.

Habit two is 'begin with the end in mind', which is quite a long habit. Since bastards only have one end in mind — personal advancement — this is not something they are likely to forget.

Habit three is 'put first things first'. Bastards will always put their own short-term interests first.

Habit four is 'think win/win'. Bastards think 'win'.

Habit five, another biggie, is 'seek first to understand, then to be understood'. Bastards cannot understand what is going on around them because they generally have no grounding in the industries in which they find themselves working. Their conviction that their 'skills' are transferable finds graduates of McDonald's University working in the media. It is impossible to understand them, because they speak as if they are continually engaged in an invisible game of American football.

Habit six is 'synergise'. Steven correctly identifies this habit, but fails to define it correctly. To synergise is to synthesise, or falsify, energy. When bastards synergise, they pretend to be focusing their efforts in a productive direction, but they are actually just trying to wangle a bigger office with a better view.

Habit seven is 'sharpen the sword' or continual self renewal. Bastards do this by changing their mind whenever their boss changes his mind, and accepting without question any new indignity placed upon them by the corporate culture.

Bearing in mind its manifest deficiencies, it is quite strange that *The Seven Habits of Highly Effective People* has been so successful.

hamburger, Australian

noun, 1. an ugly, unlovable marsupial, unrelated to the hamburger, American

The Australian hamburger is a national disgrace. I'm not talking about McDeath, or any of its franchised imitators. I'm naming and shaming the dinky-di, home-grown, chicken-shop-and-diner burger. Was it ever any good? Probably not. We ate it anyway, because there was no alternative but the Chiko Roll, and scientists had not yet gathered enough evidence to prove the Chiko Roll was a foodstuff rather than an adhesive.

The Chiko Roll is the only snack ever invented by a boilermaker, and is widely used as a sealant in the steel-fabrication trade. The hamburger, by contrast, was the creation of J. Walter Anderson, a short-order cook. J. Walter is one of the foremost Js of the 20th century, along with J. Arthur Rank of the Rank Organisation and J. Geils of the J. Geils Band.

Australian Idol-trivia-minded readers might like to know that J. Geils was the first boyfriend of *Idol* judge Marcia Hines.

I recently asked her what was his real name, and Marcia said, 'J.'

He can't have been called 'J'.

'Jay,' she said. 'J-a-y.'

Oh.

Apparently, however, she is wrong, and J was christened 'John'.

Anyway, J. Walter of Wichita, Kansas pioneered the hamburger bun. A burger without a bun is like a desert without sand, a forest without trees, or this book without **Alexander Downer**. If fast food were a magazine, the burger bun would be the covers of *Playboy*, and the patty simply the angel in the centrefold.[1]

J. Walter's invention was enthusiastically adopted by drunk blokes the world over, because you could hold it in one hand while carrying a beer in the other. Portability is the culinary attribute most favoured by drinkers, who might otherwise wander away from a sit-down meal and wrap their teeth around a brick instead.

Nobody knows how the first hamburger came to Australia, or who had the idea of inserting beetroot, but it didn't gain any flavour in transit. The Australian burger is a greasy, bland and repugnant beast, often overpowered by a soft, starchy bun and the gormless addition of a fried egg.

In the race for the face of the average drunk, the hamburger has been beaten comprehensively by its arch rival, the glorious cylindrical marsupial that is the Australian doner kebab.

When asked whether he would choose a hamburger over a kebab, the average midnight drinker replies, 'Why are you looking at my girlfriend? Didn't you steal my ferret?' then falls flat on his face.

But eating speaks louder than words, and studies show eight out of ten hungover people blame their illness on 'a dodgy kebab', even if they can't remember eating one.

Every year, a fashionable food writer, who'd rather sink his fey fork into a steaming plate of offal, happens upon a St Kilda hamburger restaurant, and is seduced by the faux '50s decor, the

---

[1] And you thought the J. Geils thing was going nowhere, didn't you?

unshaven chefs and the ordinary people dining around him. So *this* is where the masses eat, he thinks. How terribly quaint.

He goes home to write that he has found the best burger in Victoria, or Australia, or the world. And it's always bullshit. The patties are too small or too dry or too plain. The buns are too sweet or too salty or too large. The condiments are not really condiments at all, but ridiculous additions like pickled eggplant, the beetroot slices of the middle classes.

This was true until 2004, when the first Grill'd restaurant opened. Grill'd advertises its burgers as 'healthy', which would normally mean they were crap. It is a chain of franchises, which would normally mean they were double-crap. Its name is idiotically punctuated, until now a sure sign of super-double-crapness.

However, the outlet in Acland Street, St Kilda serves the best traditional hamburgers in Victoria, or Australia, or the world.

hangover cure

noun, **1.** unreliable remedy, probably worse than the disease

Mad cow disease, AIDS and the flesh-eating bug are not the only plagues sent to torment millennial man. In an effort to keep up with our apocalyptic times, the drinker's body, as it grows older, has developed a new and more terrible type of hangover. After a heavy night, I used to wake up feeling like I had been in a headbutting contest with God, and the loser had to swallow a live gerbil, but it was nothing that sweet tea and Panadol, a wank and wash would not cure. But the new kinds of hangover are more difficult to treat because they can be hard to diagnose. Often they mimic the symptoms of common, drink-related injuries such as falling down steps, being run over by cars, or getting beaten up by bouncers.

The most disturbing aspect of a mad-cow hangover is that no memory separates the night you order your second beer in Sydney from the morning you wake up in the Federated States of Micronesia. This amnesia, however, is not such a bad thing. You are unlikely to have covered yourself in glory. Although there is a tiny possibility that you'd been drinking to celebrate having sex with Britney Spears, or your surprise victory in the world chess championships, the odds are that you were trying to blot out the recollection of murdering your mother or, worse, singing in a karaoke bar.

The best thing to do when you wake up with a hangover is go back to sleep. If you cannot do this — if, for instance, it is your wedding day (and, think carefully, it might be) — you'll have to put your trust in one of the placebos, potions or paint-strippers that pass as 'hangover cures'.

Although ancient man could invent the wheel, build the pyramids, and sail the oceans without corporate sponsorship, he had no real luck with hangovers. Old English medicine suggested: 'Take the flowers of marigolds and beat them in a dish with the end of a rolling pin and wring out the juice thereof, and snuff it in your nostrils.'

In the interests of scientific research, I actually tried this, and can report that it is almost impossible to turn marigold flowers to juice by beating them. All you get is a cluster of orange petals stuck to your rolling pin. If you scrape these off and stick them up your nose, they feel surprisingly comfortable. Less surprisingly, they do nothing for your hangover. You quickly forget they are there and, every time you sneeze, you think you are having a brain haemorrhage.

Many hangover cures seem to work on the principle that if you shoot yourself in the foot, you will forget about your toothache. The foul drinks most popularly recommended for alleviating morning-after madness include the Italian Fernet Branca and the Belgian Amer Biere (Amer Picon with beer) or a tumbler of Benedictine or Grand Marnier taken with breakfast. All of these will make you feel more nauseous than the original hangover.

Many people share the misconception that a hangover is sickness brought on by poisoning yourself. In fact, it is a sickness brought on by not poisoning yourself enough: by only drinking yourself half to death.

In a flesh-eating hangover, your body is like a thug standing over your soul in the bar. You're dragging yourself up from the floor, battered and bloody, pulling tiny shards of broken glass out of your eyes and, just as you manage to pull yourself upright, Body the Thug yells, 'It ain't over yet, bro. BUY ME ANOTHER DRINK.'

And you need that drink. It does not matter if it is a Foster's or a Fernet Branca, although Foster's has the advantage of being easier to say. If you wake up feeling like a boiling death curry and immediately drink four beers, the next time you wake up you probably won't feel quite as bad, especially if you have four more beers. On the third time you open your eyes, you may still feel bad, but probably not as bad, and you only have to drink two-thirds of the previous day's ration to reach equilibrium. As a general rule, if you begin drinking heavily from the moment you open your eyes, you need never have a hangover at all.

Since this is not an option for most people with jobs, families, partners, cars, children, bladders etc, the more popular over-the-counter hangover cure remains Berocca soluble vitamin C tablets. Trendy travel agent STA recommends its backpacker clients take a tube of the stuff away with them, along with condoms and sunscreen. A Berocca-rich holiday is likely to be the kind in which your only use for the condoms is to pull them over the Berocca tube in a hilarious, bar-clearing, impress-the-babes plastic-penis impersonation — but never mind; since you'll rarely see daylight, you probably won't use the sunscreen either.

Berocca can help with a hangover, although it has a largely psychological effect. It looks like it is working. When you press to your lips the fizzing brew of tablets and water, and the tiny bubbles shoot up your nose and into your eyes, years of late-night TV suggest this should transform you from Mr Hyde back to Dr Jekyll. Even better, Berocca immediately turns your urine bright orange, creating the illusion of having coursed through your body on a mission to purify your innards, like the guys in the miniature submarine in the movie *Inner Space*.

Some sad, hungover types reach for Gatorade, a 'scientifically formulated blend of carbohydrates and electrolytes' that people believe makes you better at sports. It is safe to say that Gatorade does as much for a hangover as it does to improve overall fitness — that is, more than a road accident but less than a glass of water.

Orange Gatorade tastes exactly like orange cordial, contains many of the same ingredients (water, sugar, flavours) and costs 20 times as much. It can be bought at the corner store, but it has been priced for health-food shops, strange-smelling places where the rules of economics do not apply and a loaf of organic sourdough bread can cost $8. For hangovers, health-food shops tend to carry Amazonian Guarana powder, in difficult-to-open-when-your-fingers-are-trembling sachets. If you mix Guarana into fruit juice, as instructed, you get a glass of something that looks like mud with lava on top, and smells curiously similar to a Big Mac. Like most natural remedies, it does nothing at all. On the plus side, it does not alter the taste of the fruit juice either.

Underberg natural bitters ('world wide in the service of well-being — since 1886'), which comes in little bullet-shaped bottles sold from bandoliers in bottle shops, could also be classed a natural remedy, in that it contains 'aromatic herbs from 43 countries'. On the other hand, it is 44 per cent proof.

A favourite morning-after ministration for drinkers the world over, Underberg is quite pleasant-tasting in a cough-mixture kind of way. Whether it does anything for a hangover, other than very quickly get you drunk again, is another matter.

Overall, the best option might be to learn to love your hangover, to greet it like a friend in the morning, to wrap your thoughts in its protective coat and trust your soul to its tender care. After all, when you already feel like a corpse under a chainsaw, there is not much worse that can happen to you. An incident that would be a big thing in civilian life, such as being kidnapped by terrorists or thrown from the roof of a tall building, becomes just another boring obstacle to getting well again.

The Seven Don'ts of Highly Hungover People

Don't wrap your arm around the warm body in the bed. It is not Britney Spears. It is a horse's head, or a Scottish oil-rig worker who does not know how he got there either.

Don't wet shave without first locating your nose, which is the jutting-out thing in the middle of your face.

Don't dial the eight-digit number written on the back of your hand. It is the amount of cash you owe Chopper Read, after a bet that he would not slice off his other ear. The same person is now the legal owner of your motorbike.

Don't put on your shoes without first looking inside. They each contain half a kebab.

Don't go downstairs for a smoke, particularly if you are a non-smoker. Although there are at least three strange lighters in your pockets, there are no cigarettes. However, a bummed cigarette (try the oil-rig worker) may help you get through small but necessary tasks such as phoning your boss and putting on a funny voice to convince him you have caught 'that bug that has been going around'.

Don't bother going into detail. Your boss knows you are lying.

Don't go searching for things in the places where they are usually found. Your keys are in the fridge, your clothes are in the microwave, your car is in the swimming pool, and breakfast is in the washing machine. And anyway, this is not your house.

If the room appears to be rocking and you feel sick in the stomach, don't rush out of the door before establishing where you are. You might be on a boat.

happy slap

***noun,* 1.** violent act committed by a young **idiot**, blamed on his mobile phone by older idiots

I was lucky enough to be back in England to catch the beginning of the 2006 street-fighting season. Old Albion is at its loveliest during those long, balmy days of summer, when young men kick off their football boots, slip on their signet rings, and go out punching strangers in the street.

Unexpectedly assaulting unwary pedestrians is an English tradition as old as Morris dancing, and marginally less sickening. It has a new name, 'happy slapping', and the press says kids do it because they own camera-phones. But it was equally popular when I was at school, and telephones were attached by wires to walls.

I have many happy memories of lying on the pavement, gazing up at the stars in the night sky, bleeding from the nose and mouth, as cheery pranksters rubbed their knuckles with childlike delight.

My mate Colin was walking down the road one afternoon in 1980 when he was merrily punched on the nose by a passer-by. Weeks later, he was approached in a shopping centre by a soldier, who wanted to fight him because he had a scar on his nose.

Anyway, I was sitting outside an East End pub, drinking a pint of rubbish lager by a busy road, when I heard a crack and a whoop. I looked around to see a man lying on the floor near my feet, and three young blokes applauding. Then I realised one of them had hit him, and the others were happy because he had fallen down.

The bloke — let's call him 'the Hittee' — was in his early 20s, bewildered and upset. The Hittites, who were about the same age, were jubilant. People had been picking on the Hittee all day, his mate said.

'I've got to lose the hat,' said the Hittee, pointing to the straw trilby he appeared to blame for the violence.

'It's not the hat,' said his mate. 'It's you.'

It was the second fight I'd seen in four days. The first seemed to have been staged especially for me. While I was eating a mixed tandoori plate at a window table in an Indian restaurant in Southall, three Polish guys, including one carrying a baseball bat, chased three West Indians past the glass. I assume they were Polish because (a) every white person I met in Southall was Polish; and (b) they were dressed like op-shop dummies. The West Indians — who might equally have been Africans — were stylistically superior but lacking heavy weaponry. Nonetheless, they managed to drive the Poles back just by throwing gang signs. The Eastern Europeans quickly recovered their ground, and swooped past the window again. It was as if I were watching a reality TV show in which contestants from unlikely nations met to contest the Happy Slapping World Cup.

I never found out which team went through to meet Tuvalu in the semi-finals, because the fight rolled on up Southall Broadway and out of sight, but I felt I had reached a deeper understanding of what makes Britain great. People come from all over the world, from vastly different racial, political and religious backgrounds, but each group of new arrivals is quickly bound by the glue that holds together the nation: pointless, undirected, recreational violence.

It's as British as chips with curry sauce.

hate radio

noun, 1. type of entertainment derived from hating young people, ethnic minorities and the poor

The hate-radio announcer is a close relative of the **fright-wing columnist**. While the columnist aims to provoke fear and misunderstanding, the announcer is more explicit in seeking to foment actual hatred. He hopes that since he uses the spoken word, he leaves no easily accessible record, and will not be taken to task for anything he says.

The king of hate radio is, of course, Sydney's **Alan Jones**. Princes include Steve Price, who called for 'a community show of force' before the Cronulla race riots, and the marvellous Brian Wilshire. Around the time of the riots, Brian told his listeners that part of the problem with Middle-Eastern people in Australia is their parents are first cousins.

'The result of this is inbreeding, the result of which is uneducationable people,' he said, 'and very low IQ.'

He later apologised, but not for inventing an adjective.

Brian is deeply educationable and has a very high IQ, as is evidenced by his several brilliant books, which were among the first I read when I came to Australia in 1989. Through them, I learned 'all our financial and political problems' are the result of a 'deliberate plan laid down by those who ... profit from our misfortune'; a secret tunnel connects a bunker beneath Parliament House with the US Embassy; and an overseas-based intelligence network spies on the Australian people by means of the Telecom building in St Leonards, Sydney. Luckily, I could counter the effects of the conspiracy by immersing myself in an Epsom salts-flavoured flotation tank and inhaling hydrogen peroxide every morning. (If Brian were Alan Jones, I would suspect that he had some financial connection with the manufacturers of Epsom salts.)

Ron Casey was a master of hate radio. When he was not sure how tough the new Chinese immigrants in Chinatown might be, he said, 'It makes you feel like getting a dozen or so of your footy mates together and having a night down there — test these little bastards right out.'

His tragic downfall came when he denounced Nokia's sponsorship of the National Rugby League, in the form of the Nokia Medal. Ron believed that Nokia was a Japanese company and imagined, on air, a future where the Nokia-Medal holder might be forced to experience flashbacks to the Second World War, shouting, 'Look, I'm a POW, I'm under the Geneva rights! Oh, don't hit me over the head with the butt of your gun, you little Japanese POW guard bastard!'

When informed that Nokia is, in fact, Finnish, he apologised in cheerfully Hitlerian terms: 'They're a good European and Aryan company and I've got nothing racially against them.'

And now he is not on the radio any more.

Ron was there in spirit, however, when Alan Jones exhorted the folk of Sutherland Shire to protest against the bashing of lifeguards on Cronulla beach by a 'Lebanese gang'.

When the counter-demonstration was gaining momentum, Alan said, 'I'm the person that's led this charge here. Nobody wanted to know about North Cronulla — now it's gathered to this.'

Alan read out on the air the text message that was circulating among local youth, 'Come to Cronulla this weekend to take revenge. This Sunday every Aussie in the Shire get down to North Cronulla to support the Leb and wog bashing day.' He said he 'understood' why it went around.

It is not for nothing that race-baiter Alan has been referred to as the 'master baiter'. He even offered a suggestion for the creation of new racial divisions.

'I tell you who we want to encourage,' Alan said, 'all the Pacific Island people because … they don't take any nonsense. And they say, "Uh huh, uh huh. You step out of line, look out." And, of course, cowards always run, don't they?'

Of course, Alan warned his listeners not to take the law into their own hands. It would be unfair to suggest that some of Alan's listeners may not be the first cabs off the rank, since so many of them are taxi drivers, but it is possible they were not able to read the fine print under Alan's bold-type appeal. When the protest turned into a toy-town pogrom, and Lebanese kids were dragged off a train and bashed, Alan ran away. On holiday.

holiday snap

noun, **1.** a **happy slap** delivered by parents to defenceless children, often captured in a naked or semi-naked state

In my first holiday snap, I am nine months old, standing in a centimetre of sea water in front of a stark, pebble beach in Southport, Lancashire. There are two slightly alarming things about the photograph: (1) my head appears to be the same length as my legs; and (2) I am modelling a pair of leopard-skin-print swimming trunks. For many years, this picture sat on my mum's mantelpiece, beguiling family and visitors alike with my remarkable ability to bear my own weight at such an early age (particularly impressive considering my head must have weighed about five kilos) and my mum's remarkable ability to dress me in the worst pair of swimming trunks in the world.

I have often asked my mum why she did this to me, her first-born child. She says they must have been fashionable at the time. If this is so, how come I have never, ever seen another picture of a baby in leopard-skin-print swimming trunks, and how come everybody who looks at it shrieks, 'What on earth are you wearing?! Ha ha ha ha ha ha! Isn't that leopard skin?! Ha ha ha ha ha ha ha ha ha ha! Have you still got them?! Ha ha ha ha ha ha! Why don't you put them on now, Tarzan?! Ha ha ha ha ha! *Heur-buerg heur-burgh heur-buerg!*'

The last noise is that made by somebody struggling to breathe through a recently broken nose.

When I grew old enough to win some control over the mantelpiece, I had the leopard-skin photo consigned to a box

111

and hidden in a drawer. Every time I brought a girl home, my mum carefully opened the drawer, took the lid off the box, and killed any thought they may have had of me as a (hetero) sexual being, rather than a dwarf wrestler, or a novelty midget circus performer.

I was so traumatised by leopard-skin ridicule that there are hardly any holiday shots of me for the next 18 years — and when I first went to the beach as an adult, I wore khaki cargo pants and boxing boots. My ex-girlfriend has the pictures of this holiday, in the former Yugoslavia.

It was the only real holiday we ever had. When we next left the UK, it was to travel through Asia to Australia, and she took hundreds of pictures. When we split up, she sent me all the negatives, so I would not forget the happiest time we spent together. It has been so long since I have seen them, I don't remember what they show, except for two improbably young, frequently delighted travellers, exhilarated by the discovery of a world outside industrial England. I lost them when I moved house, as I have lost almost every memento that meant anything to me.

When I reached my mid-30s, a bloke I could barely recognise began to appear in photographs of me. He still had a faint look of me about him — but he was balder, more jowly, tubbier and grey. He was, in fact, my dad, which was all the more remarkable since he had died ten years previously.

For several holidays, I ducked for cover every time a camera came out. I didn't want to have to talk people through a series of inexplicable images: 'There's the ghost of my father drinking with my girlfriend in Thailand', 'There's the ghost of my father wearing my clothes and carrying my backpack'.

My holiday snaps became all landscape, no portrait; all statue, no head.

I moved across the world to get away from the leopard-skin photo, but it found me in Sydney, when my brother had it duplicated, enlarged, mounted (in a leopard-yellow frame, of course) and sent to my partner for Christmas.

A strange thing has happened, though. I can look at it with joy, and love in my heart, because it now appears to be a picture of my baby son. The lad in the leopard skin has his eyes, his hair, his smile. The only difference is, his mother has got far more taste than to dress him up like custom upholstery in a Monaro and plonk him on the foreshore. Are you listening, Mum? ARE YOU LISTENING?

Holocaust denier

noun, 1. Nazi

You don't really believe the Holocaust didn't happen, you sick, perverted concentration-camp wank-fantasist. You know exactly what the Nazis did, but you think they did not do enough of it, and you would like somebody more thorough (you, maybe) to have another go.

So why don't you just come out and say that, instead of drawing your stupid diagrams?

Howard hater

***noun,* 1.** reality avoider

A friend once said to me, 'Who votes Liberal? I don't know anyone who votes Liberal,' as if elections were a sham like the trial of Joh Bjelke-Petersen, and the Young Liberals were stuffing the ballot box.

I don't vet people's voting intentions before they sit down at my table — although perhaps I should — but I'd guess that I hardly know anyone who does not vote Liberal. They mostly have good jobs, nice houses, private health care, and perhaps a few shares. They are not robbed by rising interest rates or cowed by mass unemployment. They are doing fine, and they want to continue to do fine.

They are not in thrall to a charismatic conservative demagogue. John Howard is no Che Guevara. He is a poster on no one's bedroom wall. As a person, he barely even exists. Who can remember anything he ever said? Who has ever seen the prime minister and a bowling ball with a ferret strapped to each side in the same room together? John Howard is a mood, he is a feeling. He is boring. He is nasty. He is unprincipled. But the voters don't want Gough Whitlam, they want a bank manager.

They want everybody in society to abide by the rules, but they don't want to be told what to do by a Hitler or a Stalin. They prefer an authority figure with the charisma and menace of a tram conductor. John Howard is not a demagogue, he is not a dictator, he is not a 'fascist' (oh, please), but he is a liar, and he is a bastard. He pretends to be on the side of the 'battlers' — he cannot say the word 'workers' — but he has done as much as he can to keep down wages, while 'compensation' for the injurious task of being a company **CEO** has risen faster than a speeding judge.

John Howard justified WorkChoices' dismantling of the award system because the economy was so healthy that employees had won the upper hand over employers. This was at a time when *The Economist*, the employers' own house magazine, editorialised that, in the developed world, 'labour's share of GDP has fallen to historic lows, while profits are soaring'.[1] John knows this, and that is why he is a bastard.

Fright-wing columnists like to say that left-wingers who hate John Howard actually hate the people who vote for him, as if this were a logically untenable position. But left-wingers don't hate Liberal voters — in part because they don't believe Liberal voters exist — they hate the things they think Liberal voters believe.

They think Liberals hate refugees, for instance, but most Liberal voters wish refugees no ill. In fact, Liberals hope life is good for people who live overseas, so that they do not want to come here. They don't hate Muslims — they did not even know what they were until recently — but they don't want Islamists running the show.

Liberal voters have what they need — the mortgage, the 4WD, the big TV — and they are determined to keep hold of it. No ragtag bunch of sinking-boat people is going to throw their

---

[1] 'Rich Man, Poor Man', *The Economist*, 20/01/07, p11.

children overboard to swim to the shore and unplug *their* Foxtel connection. And the poorer the Liberal voters are, the less they have, the more they are concerned that criminals or immigrants (or, worst of all, immigrant criminals) will come along and take it from them.

The unions cannot defend their interests — the unions can't even defend themselves — so they look to a tram conductor with ferrets on his head to ensure an orderly queue.

John Howard's government will come to an end. It's probably on its way out now.

When he has gone, he will, like Margaret Thatcher, be widely reviled for having presided over a 'nasty' government that made citizens feel mean-spirited and small-minded. His economic achievements will be grudgingly accepted — and the Labor Party won't overturn his industrial relations legislation — but people will grumble that he could have been more gentle, more caring, a kindly grandfather rather than a harsh stepfather. The fright-wing columnists will disappear, or reinvent themselves as more sophisticated, more nuanced, kinder and nicer. They will say that the Labor Party has changed, not they. John Howard will become a straw man, a scapegoat, a story told to children to warn them against the folly of following the bland. He will be routinely dismissed as an intellectual lightweight, an unthinking supporter of the US, a one-eyed economic rationalist. At first, **Alexander Downer** and Tony Abbott will write angry letters to the press, defending his reputation from every slight, fighting a rearguard action against left-wing historical revisionism, then they too will fade away. John Howard will be discredited and ridiculed, frozen out of his own party. And, like Margaret Thatcher, nobody will ever admit to having voted for him.

human resources

noun, 1. an alien waste of resources, **people persons** from the planet Zog

Of all the pseudo-professions, 'human resources management' is the most pseudo- and least professional. It used to be called personnel management, but that was not a big enough title for people whose job was at the vanguard of doing nothing useful while drawing a salary.

The HR profession is the fount of much meaningless language and idiotic neologism. It has given us benchmarks and behavioural criteria, learning organisations and leadership, **performance appraisals** and presenteeism.

Young workers often believe the human resources department engages in a kind of corporate social work, acting as a neutral arbiter between management and employees. In reality, it is a police force for the bosses, enforcing idiotic rules (on behalf of both the company and the government) and ensuring disputes are solved to the benefit of the employer.

It has certain other nominal functions, centred around 'learning', but these are largely window dressing. The department cannot train most people because it does not understand their functions, which is why it believes abseiling is a useful skill in most office jobs.

Much of HR time is spent obscuring HR's purpose with difficult-to-understand emails.

The recruitment industry is the military wing of HR. Its operations are highly complex, and not easily understood by an untrained lay person.

In a revealing interview in the *Sydney Morning Herald*,[1] Matt Gribble, the NSW director of recruitment firm Michael Page International, attempted to explain to the layman the complexities of his exacting profession. How, for instance, might a candidate for a job demonstrate that he or she is 'a team player'?

'Showing they played team sports or worked as a part of a team ... would lend weight to a candidate's claim they are a team player,' he said.

Give that man a pay rise!

---

[1] Careers and Employment Expo, *Sydney Morning Herald*, 26/07/02, p8.

identity thief

noun, 1. credit-card thief, upgraded in the criminal hierarchy in recent years, perhaps because (a) people now consider their credit card to be their identity; or (b) their crime can be committed over the internet, which makes them much more scary to older people, who generally have yet to figure out how email works

My mum is often first with the latest warnings. When I phoned her before we came to visit her in England, she reminded me to keep my baby son away from document shredders.

'*They're dangerous,*' she said.

No worries. I don't have a document shredder.

'Ah,' said Mum, 'but I've got two.'

Well, perhaps we ought to stay in Australia, then.

My mum shreds her documents (whatever *they* might be) to shield herself from identity theft. It's unclear who would want my mum's identity, what with her bad back and everything, but the UK newspapers paint a stark picture of a nation divided into have-identities and have-nots. On the one side lurk those fools who were frivolous with their identities, allowed criminals unshredded access to their personal details, and thus lost everything. They live on as sad, listless zombies, wandering from post office to pie shop, unsure whether they are Nelson Mandela or Thomas the Tank Engine. On the other side of the divide sit cautious folk who eat their phone bills and never buy anything over the internet. They have more identities than Dr Jekyll, due to their identity frugality.

My mum has long felt under threat from the criminal classes, and is always careful to keep one step ahead of them. Her kitchen door, for example, carries six different locks, although half its surface area is covered by a plain glass window, and another significant section by a cat flap.

The last time Mum was burgled, criminal masterminds smashed the front window and climbed into the living room. Luckily, however, they took the DVD player, not Mum's identity.

Mentally ill people (of which my mum is not one) have usually stood at the vanguard of the identity-defence movement, protecting their minds (and, often, their anuses) from alien encroachment, by use of such devices as tin-foil skullcaps. I have spoken to psychologists (in a personal rather than professional capacity) who tell me that the walking mad no longer believe they are Napoleon Bonaparte (if they ever did). They are more likely to be of the opinion that they are Osama bin Laden, or somebody who knows him, and they often have some vital information to offer about al-Qaeda's terrorist plans.

I met a novelty wedding celebrant, who will take on any identity requested of him. He presided over an Osama bin Laden–themed wedding, organised by a couple from Western Australia. Dressed in robes, turban and false beard, he held a toy gun to the head of the groom, and threatened, 'Marry her, or I'll kill you.' He then pulled back his poncho to reveal a suicide-bomb belt.

Yet you never hear Osama railing against 'Zionists, Crusaders, wedding celebrants and identity thieves'. I guess he calculates that the more Osamas there are, the less chance there is that the Americans will get the right one. After all, the US invaded secular Iraq, rather than militantly theocratic Iran, to stop the spread of Islamic fundamentalism. It is as if Iraq had stolen Iran's identity. Or vice versa.

If Iceland were ever to attack the US (like Iraq didn't) and I happened to live in Ireland (like I don't) I would be deeply worried. It must be bad enough in Bagdad, Tasmania.

idiot

***noun*, 1.** an uneducationable person[1]

Not all idiots are bastards, and many bastards are not idiots, but there is a degree of overlap. The actual percentile is difficult to

---

[1] With thanks to Brian Wilshire.

determine, because several prominent bastards, such as **hate-radio** announcers and **fright-wing columnists**, may pretend to be idiots to connect with the broader idiot population. There are fewer idiots than the master baiters believe, but they remain a force in our society. Pauline Hanson, as previously noted, is an idiot but not a bastard, while **Philip Ruddock** is a bastard but not an idiot.

Idiots are characterised by their willingness to believe anything, from advertorial to L. Ron Hubbard. Many are fond of **conspiracy theories**, which they use to explain the bad luck that has dogged their lives. Middle-class idiots join the **non-productive professions** en masse, and have achieved a near monopoly in **marketing**. Working-class idiots spend much of their time calling hate radio stations. Upper-class idiots may be members of the **British royal family**, or associated colonial hangers-on.

It would be a mistake to believe all idiots are uneducated. Many came up through the School of Hard Knocks and took a degree at the University of Life. They may even have submitted a PhD to the Department of Banging your Head Against a Brick Wall Until your Eyes Bleed. A large number also choose to study for a Bachelor of Business at Bond University, and more than one has gone on to author a textbook on time management.

Jones, Alan

proper noun, **1.** whatever you pay him to be

Alan Jones is a Sydney-based broadcaster who has never made an issue of his sexuality, except once in a public toilet in London, and that has never been proven.

Alan is very angry about something, but it is hard to pick what or why. He seems to be perfectly comfortable with his sexuality, which is why he has never made it an issue. The fact that Alan is gay should never be mentioned again, for this and one other reason: if his listeners knew for certain, *they might not like him any more.*

Homosexual **fright-wing columnist** Christopher Pearson suggested leftists who supported the outing of Alan Jones were guilty of 'selective homophobia', even when, like David Marr, they were homosexual themselves. This was one of the more curious claims made by the press pack of 'Alan's-a-victim'-whining, chardonnay-sipping, latte-drinking, cheese-eating, soon-to-announce-surrender-in-Iraq monkeys that gathered to defend Alan against the indignity of having a biography written about him.

It would be different if Alan dressed as a suburban housewife and delivered his whining denunciations in a silly, high voice. His listeners would squeal with outraged jollity if campy Alan had said, 'David might be scraping the bottom of the barrel here, but he certainly won't be scraping *my* bottom with *his* barrel.'

But Alan does not talk or behave like a pantomime pillow-biter. He acts like an ordinary man who wears a suit and tie and loves sport and sportspeople and baiting minorities, when he is an undeclared member of a sexual minority himself, and there is something sinister there that any self-identified battler can recognise.

Most of the fright-wing columnists and their friends in radio say, to some extent, what they are paid to say. Few are as one-dimensional as they make out. Some of the columnists cannot write. For them, their most saleable skill is their willingness to make themselves lucratively unpopular. Alan's career has followed the logic of mercenary journalism to its logical end. He is **advertorial** made flesh. For years, he did not declare his sponsors, and he spoke their messages in the same warm, practiced tone he used to praise worthy battlers and Pauline Hanson. He did not pause between his heartfelt denouncements of Aboriginal people and heartfelt endorsements of Qantas and Telstra. He was bastardry nonpareil.

juncture, at this

noun, **1.** ever. Eg 'The minister will not comment about the allegations at this juncture', ie the minister will never admit anything, ever

key card

noun, 1. a plastic card that does not open the door to a hotel room, or does so only occasionally

It was an unhappy day for travel writers when the great hotels of the world got together and conspired to replace door keys with key cards. I understand why they did it — after all, I was the guest who continually left with the room key in his back pocket (and the room fixtures in his bag) — but they might have waited until they got the technology sorted out.

Key cards, like **public relations consultants**, are pieces of intelligent plastic. Each time a guest checks in, a member of the hotel staff inserts a random card into a device that impregnates it with the details of the guest's room. There are no marks on the card to indicate the room number, which is usually scribbled on a flimsy paper wallet. I always throw this wallet away. Therefore, I never have any record of my room number, and I am generally convinced that it is the number of the last room I stayed in, which was always in another hotel and often in another country. This last number was generally drummed into my head because of the number of times I had to go down to reception and report the fact that my key card was faulty.

About ten per cent of key cards never work. You pick them up from the desk, travel up in the elevator to your bedroom, insert the card six different ways into the electronic lock, and the light does not turn green. Eighty per cent of key cards check out before you do, generally while you are making one final visit to the hotel gym, and leave you sweating in your tracksuit in the corridor outside your room, trying to convince the maid that you are a guest, even though you are dressed and behaving like a junkie. The remaining ten per cent of key cards are so powerful that they neutralise the little black strip on your credit card, rendering you unable to pay your bill.

I realise, however, there is never going to be any great public sympathy for the plight of travel writers, and even if we were all wiped out at once — if, for instance, a tsunami hit a five-star resort where we were all freeloading together, under the guise of a 'conference' or 'famil' — the subsequent appeal would be lucky to raise the price of 200 duty-free cigarettes.

Ah, you readers are a bunch of heartless bastards.

learning curve

noun, **1.** learning

Lack of brevity is the source of witlessness. No bastard would ever use one word where four would do. Bastards never simply learn things any more. They are always 'on a learning curve'. The idea appeals to them because it sounds scientific, the sort of thing they might be able to demonstrate with a **PowerPoint presentation**.

Most bastards have the concept of a learning curve backwards. The idea is simple: as you do something more often, you get better at it, and the relationship between practice and proficiency can be expressed, diagrammatically, in a curve.

Bastards seem to have developed the idea that a learning curve is something you climb, and the narrower the gradient, the more difficult the knowledge is to acquire. When they say they are on a 'steep learning curve', they are trying to say they are finding something difficult. Actually, if mastering a new skill involved a steep learning curve, that skill would be comparatively easy to attain.

Bastards are unnaturally interested in curves in general. It was bastards who invented the Bell Curve, which was supposed to show black people were thicker than white people, even Pauline Hanson. When confronted with a question they cannot answer, bastards will often refer to that query as a curved or curve ball, or even a 'curvy one'. This is because (a) it is a metaphor derived from the bastard's favourite source, the game of baseball; and (b) they are stupid.

Liechtenstein

proper noun, 1. a small European nation set up to fleece tourists at the petrol pumps

Do not fill up your car at the service station in Schaan, Liechtenstein. It sells the most expensive petrol in Europe, if not the world. Although the sign offers fuel at $2.20 per litre (about AUD$56 for three-quarters of a tank), it is charged back to your credit card at the conveniently rotund sum of $100.

The entire transaction is automated. There is no attendant at the garage. You simply slot your credit card in a machine, fill the tank, do not receive a receipt because you can't read the instructions in German, and find out you were charged $4 a litre when your Visa bill arrives a month later.

Fill up your car in rural Austria instead. The official price is lower there, anyway.

In fact, the price of everything is lower in rural Austria, with the possible exception of wholesale false teeth, of which Liechtenstein is the world's largest manufacturer. The smiling Ivoclar Vivadent false-teeth factory sits in a valley between green hills, like dentures resting in the bottom of a glass.

The tiny principality of Liechtenstein is a collection of 11 villages with a total population of about 34,000. Its neighbours are Austria and Switzerland, its language is German, its scenery is Alpine, and its lax banking laws have turned it into a world centre for money laundering.

Tourists go to Liechtenstein to get a stamp in their passports, an opportunity that is becoming increasingly rare in a Europe *sans frontieres*. The government has cottoned on to this, and charges $2.20 for the service. You cannot get stamps at the border — where, incidentally, an Australian driving licence is accepted as sufficient identification — but they are available from the tourist office in the capital village, Vaduz.

An unkind person with a petrol-based grudge might be tempted to comment that passport-stamping is the full extent of Liechtenstein's tourism industry — but that would ignore the Museum of Calculators, also in the cursed village of Schaan.

The Museum of Calculators was closed when we reached

Liechtenstein. Visitors are by appointment only, presumably to prevent the dangerous overcrowding that would otherwise occur. Luckily, however, Liechtenstein's Postage Stamp Museum is open seven days a week. A narrow-minded, faintly embittered commentator might claim the only interesting thing about the world's fourth-smallest country is its colourful and varied output of stamps. It is as if they don't even know about the Museum of Calculators! Which, as I say, was closed.

Liechtenstein's interesting and varied past is chronicled in the National Museum of Liechtenstein, whose permanent collection shows what was happening in Liechtenstein in Neolithic times (nothing) through Medieval times (nothing) to the present (nothing). The building also holds more specialised temporary exhibitions, and I was lucky enough to catch a fascinating presentation about the history of the National Museum of Liechtenstein.

It was 7pm when I checked in at the Gastof Au, in Vaduz, and an old guy was already asleep at the bar. Another bunch of retirees, all of whom seemed to have been cut from the same potato, had come out for an evening of staring at things. They took a long, blank gape at my girlfriend and me as we carried our luggage into reception.

Outside, a goat grazed by a block of units, and cows nuzzled trees alongside the main road. Snow-capped alps looked down boredly on green fields and scrappy buildings.

At dusk, the pedestrian-only Stadtl, the heart of Vaduz, throbbed to the beat of *When I'm 64* played on a distant Wurlitzer organ, and passionate applause greeted the stirring chords of *Dam Busters March*.

We ate at the Restaurant bar Vinothek, where the waiter said, 'Thank you for being here.'

I asked for a local beer to accompany my pasta, but he said the closest they had was Eldeplez Schutzengarden, brewed 80 kilometres away in Switzerland.

In the nearby bars, young Liechtenstanis partied until the early hours. At the trendy Black Box (open until 3am) I was not game enough to try to pronounce 'Eldeplez Schutzengarden', so I pointed to a beer and asked for 'one of those'.

'No,' said the barmaid, firmly. 'This is a man's. He has gone to the toilet.'

I didn't actually mean… Oh, never mind.

On Saturday morning, Stadtl was deserted. It was as if everybody had left for Austria, to fill up with petrol. We wandered the streets (well, street, really) until lunchtime, when we ate cheap, tasty Asian food at Leah's Eiscream & Philippen Imbiss.

I asked Leah if Vaduz ever gets any livelier.

'No,' she said. 'Remember, this is Liechtenstein.'

life coach

noun, **1.** anybody who calls himself a life coach

A coach is a vehicle that takes you from one place to another in maximum discomfort, via a number of places you do not want to go, for a ticket that costs the same as a discount economy airfare. A life coach is like a coach, but without reclining seats. An **executive coach** is like a life coach, but at the price of a business-class fare.

According to the University of Sydney's Anthony Grant, life coaching is 'a collaborative solution-focused, results-orientated and systematic process in which the coach facilitates the enhancement of work, performance, life experience, self-directed learning and personal growth of the coachee'.

That, really, is all you need to know. Anybody can be a life coach; there is no trade qualification because it is not a trade. If you are tempted to consult a life coach, you might as well reach your decisions by reading fortune cookies.

Little Britain

proper noun, **1.** transvestite television, or TV TV

I was in the heart of London's Little Australia, watching the *Little Britain* stage show in a theatre full of little British people (and some big ones). I was sitting with my British little brother, who was excited we had tickets to the sell-out show. He was a mild fan, and I was hoping he could explain *Little Britain*'s appeal to me.

Like the rest of the audience at the Carling Hammersmith Apollo, my brother had heard all the jokes before, because the

Little Britain TV series has exactly the same number of gags as it has regular characters.

Identical things happen to each person in every sketch in which they appear. Grotesque, ridiculously dressed Daffyd Thomas, who believes he is 'the only gay in the village' is blind to the evidence of homosexuality in everyone else around him. Grotesque, ridiculously dressed transvestite Emily Howard says, 'I'm a laaaady,' then does something unladylike. Grotesque, ridiculously dressed Maggie Blackamoor vomits when she comes into contact with minorities or anything they might have touched. Grotesque, ridiculously dressed criminal single mother Vicky Pollard, caught committing an offence, tries to talk her way out of trouble with inarticulate, repetitive babble. Grotesque, ridiculously dressed Bubbles Devere, a fat, bald woman, takes off her clothes and wig, and tries to act seductive.

But the Little Britishers loved it. They laughed at every punchline, even though they knew it was coming from the moment the sketch began. Every time I asked my brother why a particular action was funny, he said, 'It's because they always do that.'

When the stage show opened in London, the curtain rose, and a disembodied voice announced an evening in which men would dress up as women and act gay. Most of *Little Britain's* female characters are played by its co-stars and creators, David Walliams and Matt Lucas. Matt is gay, David is not, but they make equally attractive transvestites. Like all cross-dressing male entertainers, from Fatty Vautin — from rugby league's *Footy Show* — to Barry Humphries, the core of their joke is: Aren't women absurd! They speak in silly, high voices! They wear funny, floral clothes! They have trivial, small-minded concerns! To this, the *Little Britain* team add: Aren't fat women revolting! Aren't poor women stupid! Aren't rural women bigoted! And so much more.

Little Britain's rhythms, cadences and reference points come from Blackpool pier pantomimes, where faded male entertainers saw out their twilight years, overmade up in oversize frocks, and rising young women strapped down their breasts and pretended to be boys. To appeal to adults as well as children, the familiar, simplistic plots were layered with national servicemen's innuendo and footie club double entendre; the villains were as camp as bush tea, and always 'behiiiiiiiind you'.

Generations of little British children — including me — were raised on this seaside-postcard humour, but I seem to be the only one who has grown out of it. The rest of the audience laughed like a baby who sees a parent's hand poised to tickle. It giggles in happy anticipation of familiar pleasure. Oh, the transvestite's going to vomit! Oh, the transvestite's going to wet herself! Oh, the transvestite's going to undress down to her fat suit!

In homage to another pantomime tradition, members of the *Little Britain* audience are pulled from their seats and onto the stage. One young man played a game of 'hide the sausage', during which he was mounted by Walliams, who was pretending to be an aggressive homosexual. Walliams tore at his trousers. Oh look! He's simulating anal rape! In a later scene, a pregnant woman was brought to the front and told she looked ridiculous.

I could not believe the young guy was a genuine, paying customer, but he went to the bar at the intermission and drank a beer with his girlfriend. He did not seem insulted, violated, or even embarrassed. Maybe I should just lighten up.

In the second part of the *Little Britain* show, there were a couple of really funny bits: understated, apparent ad libs, where David and Matt played off each other with an unforced battery of jokes about (sigh) anal sex. For the most part, though, it is *Viz* comics brought to life with the irony rendered invisible by misanthropic zeal. It feels like middle-class men looking down on the lower orders; a private schoolboys' end of term review, in which the prefects mock their cook, their gardener and their classmates' vulgar mothers.

As we filed out of the Carling Hammersmith Apollo with the Little British, most of them smiling and exchanging some variation on, 'That was great, that was,' I challenged my brother again. Why did he like it?

'I suppose it's not *that* funny,' he said, crestfallen.

I felt as though I had stolen something from him, so I didn't say anything more.

loop, the

noun, 1. paradise. **noun, 2.** An 8mm pornographic movie

No bastard ever wants to be outside the loop, because the loop is such a wonderful place to be. The sun is always shining inside the loop, and pretty girls chase butterflies while strapping young men bathe in sylvan glades to the strains of **classical music**. Outside the loop, an icy breeze blows, and pathetic, naked wretches tear each other's limbs off in the struggle to reach the small shelter afforded by dank, shallow caves. When the victors grow old and weak, they are tossed out into the elements by their own ungrateful children, and die in agony as crows peck out their eyes.

In the days before video killed the peep-show booth star, the term 'loop' referred to cheap, usually silent, pornographic shorts, generally viewed 'on a loop' by paying customers in sex shops. The most famous of these showed Linda Lovelace having sex with a greyhound.

Bastard-busting tip number five: The next time your **brand** manager asks, 'Can you keep me in the loop?' reply, 'Certainly. Do you want to be Linda or the dog?'

lunchtime drinking

noun, **1.** very poor idea that is inevitably the source of even worse ideas. Eg 'I went lunchtime drinking with the **HR manager**, and told him *exactly* what I thought of him. Now I am between jobs'

I don't drink at lunchtime. Only two kinds of people drink at lunchtime: alcoholics and non-drinkers. By 'non-drinkers', I mean the folk who can 'pop out for a quick one' and not come back four days later married to a Samoan transvestite they met in a police cell in St Kilda.

When I say I don't drink at lunchtime, I don't mean I *never* drink at lunchtime. That would be fanaticism. On one occasion I *had* to drink at lunchtime, because I had an interview for a job on the telly. My friend Jack Marx also had an interview — same morning, same job — and we had to go to the pub afterwards to talk about it. Obviously.

That day I also had a meeting (they don't seem to be called 'appointments' any more) with Ian 'Dicko' Dickson — who already had a job on the telly — in a pub in North Sydney. Once I was there, it seemed logical to continue drinking.

As a result, I had downed nine beers by 5pm, and quickly lost my patience trying to flag a taxi home. With a drunk's peculiar conviction that travelling anywhere is better than standing still, I jumped on a passing bus to Kings Cross, even though I was going to Newtown. I headed southeast to get southwest, as if I were trying to shake off a pursuer. My rationale — if I can call it that — was there are always lots of cabs in Kings Cross. For reasons I don't understand, I didn't have to pay a bus fare.

When I arrived in Kings Cross, I stumbled into a newsagency to check out the magazines.

I was followed by a junkie prostitute hissing, 'Do you want a girl?'

Why, yes. That's why I'm in a newsagency.

Eventually I found my way back to Newtown, but two weeks later I was back in the Cross, sitting in Cafe Tropicana, when a coat-hanger-shouldered, twitching, swearing heroin addict — who showed every sign of having been drinking at lunchtime — was gently removed from the property. Once he was a safe distance away, he assumed the position and shouted the usual challenges to come out and fight him on the street. For the first time in the long and colourful history of junkies being ejected from cafes, somebody actually took him literally and punched him out.

At a Kings Cross newsagency, a different woman asked, 'Do you want a *lady*?' as if my earlier reticence might have been due to the age of the junkie on offer.

Just a magazine, thanks.

I then went into a sex shop to look for a copy of the Paris Hilton sex tape, which I hoped to 'review' in the rehearsal for the TV show. (I still didn't have the role, but I'd moved up a stage in the selection process.) I climbed down some stairs to premises below street level, fully expecting somebody to try to sell me a newspaper.

I passed beneath an inflatable sheep, its box inviting, 'Pull the wool and jam the lamb ... I love ewe so much,' to find *1 Night in Paris* costs $79.95 — twice the average for an X-rated DVD. I didn't buy it, in part because I wasn't sure if you could claim something illegal as a tax deduction. I've no such worries about lunchtime drinking. As any businessperson will tell you, it's always a work-related expense.

Kings Cross has never shaken off the sex and drugs trades, despite the council's fantastic idea of getting rid of streetwalkers and street people by *making the pavement wider*. St Kilda, however — where the pavements are as wide as they've ever been — no longer seems the kind of place where you can walk past a heavily tattooed dwarf, or into a bar where a woman shouts 'Do you want to see my vagina?' and then shows you — both of which happened to me on the same day in the old millennium.

I've never had a lunchtime drink in St Kilda. Well, not never — that would be fanaticism — but not for a while. The last time I was approached in the Acland Street newsagency, it was by an English backpacker, who asked me if I knew where there was an orthodox synagogue where he might get a free Friday night feed.

No, I'm sorry, I don't. I only come into newsagencies to pick up women.

marketing

***noun*, 1.** advertising oneself

'Marketing is "the means by which mutually beneficial exchanges occur,"' Mark Crowe, **CEO** of the Australian Marketing Institute, told the *Sydney Morning Herald* in 2006.

This could be a useful definition of anything from consensual sexual intercourse to professional lawn tennis, but it does not describe the work of the bastard who sits in the marketing department, furthering his own career at the expense of the productive people around him.

Marketing people often claim to be concerned with the Four Ps: Product, Pricing, Promotion and Placement. Actually, their main considerations are Playing Politics, Pandering, Promotion-Seeking and **Passion**-Feigning.

There is nothing wrong with marketing as such (in fact, if this book does not become a bestseller, it will be entirely because it has been marketed incorrectly), but there is something disturbing about the people who see a career in marketing primarily as a chance to market themselves.

Watch them closely, because they will piss in your mouth and tell you a mutually beneficial exchange has occurred.

marzipan

noun, **1.** horrible surprise, hiding under icing

Biting into a cake and discovering a layer of marzipan is like putting your hand up a woman's skirt and finding a penis. Unless you are a gay man, in which case it is like putting your hand up a woman's skirt and not finding a penis. Either way, it's hardly the sort of stuff you would want on a birthday cake.

me

pronoun, **1.** journalist and author, largely unknown

I am a continual and predictable disappointment to myself. Despite my best efforts to live in the moment, I never forget anything, apart from where I left my iPod, what time my flight leaves, the importance of personal hygiene etc. Every grudge and slight and chance encounter with a bastard lives on in my mind as if it happened moments ago.

I am always trying to pull a fast one on myself, to slip one by me while my attentions are elsewhere. I make excuses for not doing what I know I need to do, and to justify spending time on something easier instead. I write books criticising **fridge magnet**s when I could be working on the Great Australian Novel. I spend hours investigating what became of the Wilderness Society koala people while my colleagues write award-winning pieces of investigative journalism exposing corruption in high places.

I never manage to quit drinking for long and, when I start again, I quickly make up for every beer I missed. I talk back to presidents and prime ministers on TV, even though I am fairly sure they cannot hear me. I waste time reading **advertorial**s, particularly when they promise **baldness** cures, but have never read anything written in 19th century Russia.

I have allowed, even encouraged, advertorial in magazines I have edited. However, I believe that, if I comb my few remaining hairs with sufficient care and attention to detail, I will not look bald. Every year, I put off learning Chinese, with the idea that it will be easier when I am older.

In my last book, I claimed my dad could not read until he was 30. My mum tells me he could read, just not very well, because he was dyslexic. I also said my grandparents had burned my mum's O-level certificate, whereas in fact it was my auntie's they had threatened to burn. They only told my mum she was not to continue at school. These are quite important points, since nobody else is ever likely to write a book about my dad or my mum.

I am proud to be a journalist, but there is something a bit iffy about journalism. Everyone you interview thinks you are going to write a story about how wonderful they are, whereas no editor ever says, 'Write a story about this guy and how wonderful he is,' unless they are talking about a friend of the proprietor.

I hate it when people ask, 'What's your angle?' but it is a legitimate question and I would ask it myself if a journalist wanted to interview me.

I wish my stories were kinder, and added a little more to people's understanding of themselves and others, and I wish I could think up more jokes about **Alexander Downer**.

mecca

noun, **1.** any place any group of people might go for any reason

Mecca is a city in **Saudi Arabia** which Muslims believe to be the holiest place on earth. Every Muslim with the means to do so is expected to make a pilgrimage to Mecca (or hajj) once in his or her lifetime, during the Islamic month of Dhu al-Hijja. Traditionally, once they arrive, there is a major disaster and hundreds of people die.

The idea that many people could want to go to the same place at once has a very powerful pull on the minds of imbeciles. They believe it is okay to call anything a 'mecca' if it attracts crowds of like-minded folk. Kings Cross, Bondi and the Whitsunday Islands are each regularly described as a 'mecca' for tourists or backpackers. Often a mecca is a place where large numbers of young people go to have sex and get drunk. I doubt this is what takes place on the hajj (although there is probably more of it than the Saudis let on).

Saudi Arabia, as I have mentioned, is our unflinching ally in the War Against Terror, and for peaceful coexistence between Muslims, Christians and Jews. Therefore, the entire actual city of Mecca is permanently closed to non-Muslims, except in 1979 when Islamic fundamentalists opposed to the Islamic fundamentalist government of the Al-Saud family occupied the Grand Mosque, and the Saudis invited in the French anti-terrorist police to kill hundreds of devout Muslims.

Therefore, 'a mecca for backpackers', for example, would be closed to package tourists, except when a load of other backpackers invited the French in to kill them all.

This is unlikely to happen in the Whitsundays.

media basher

noun, **1.** person who knows what is going on in the world instinctively, without reference to newspapers, CNN etc

I wear a sign on my head that says 'Talk to me'. Due to a process I do not understand, it is only visible to stupid people, and only after they have consumed ten tinnies of VB. I was walking through a country town once when a flushed, fat man called me over to the bus stop, where he was boring two women who could not escape because they were waiting for a bus.

He did not understand why I was on my own (a problem stupid people often have) and invited me to join him, his wife and the two strangers at the bus stop. I told him I was a journalist, and I saw the midgets in his mechanical mind get to work pulling their levers.

He was trying to say, 'Never let the truth get in the way of a good story, eh?' but he could not find the words. Eventually, he managed, 'As long as it's a good story.'

'Yes,' I agreed. 'We make everything up. And what job do you do, mate?'

I was using the inflected 'mate' in its country-town sense, as a synonym for female genitalia.

His wife stepped in to say something anodyne about how much she had enjoyed a travel story she read that morning. I asked my question again, but the bloke did not seem to understand. Or perhaps he had no job, and could not get one because he could not accept that the vacancies advertised in the newspaper were real.

It amazes me how many people apparently believe the news is invented by journalists. What are the sources of their superior knowledge of world affairs? Do they doubt there is a war in Iraq? Do they doubt there is a place called Iraq? Do they honestly think there is no substantial difference between *SBS News* and *Bananas in Pyjamas*? Or is media cynicism just a way by which unsophisticated people, such as the lazily named Senator **Santo Santoro**, affect a veneer of worldliness?

meeting

noun, **1.** group of bastards. **2.** any two bastards together in the same place

The natural habitat of bastards is the meeting. When you phone them, they are invariably 'in a meeting', because bastards have managed to push the definition of a meeting to include any kind of human interaction. If they are having a conversation with another person, it is, de facto, a meeting. If that other person is a bastard too, it is a high-level meeting.

messenger bag

noun, 1. school satchel

That's a nice bag, Mr Management Consultant. It looks really great slung over the shoulder of your suit jacket. You must have some very important stuff in there. Like maybe a catapult, a pocket knife, and a Christmas beetle in a matchbox.

I think maybe you got up this morning and accidentally picked up your son's satchel. Imagine his surprise when he gets to school and unpacks a **PowerPoint presentation** detailing the rightsizing of outsourcing in an upskilled world, and a brown-paper package of Dutch farmyard porn.

If, however, that is your own satchel you are carrying, I suggest you jazz it up a bit by writing in marker pen the name of your favourite football team or pop band, or having everyone in your year-eight class autograph the flap.

Then you will look really cool, and all the chicks in the office will want to pash you.

P.S. What have you got for lunch? Milo sandwiches?

no brainer

***noun*, 1.** question, the answer to which is considered obvious by people with no brains

A good example of a no brainer is: 'How do we make the world safe from terrorism?' Brainless respondents will reply, 'Invade Iraq.'

numberplates, personalised

***noun*, 1. fridge magnet** for an ego

old age

***noun,* 1.** youth with a hangover

I used to think live music was the most magnificent, exhilarating and terrifying thing in the world. Before I was 16, I had seen The Clash, The Jam, The Buzzcocks and a lump of other punk bands whose once-shocking haircuts are now imitated by bank clerks, advertising salespeople, and **Downer**-voting, sanctions-busting, Saddam-subsidising wheat farmers from Mayo.

I used to push myself to the front of the crowd until my chest was pressed against the stage, and dance a spiky, constricted pogo to avoid being crushed to death. All around me, bigger men were spitting at the band, groping girls, and cheerfully punching each other in the face, in the time-honoured manner of English people out to enjoy themselves.

These days, I have become more dependent on furniture to have a good time. When recently I went to see Steve Earle — a US 'alt country' singer who is as punk as a man can be at 51 — I chose a club that had tables and chairs, so I might be able to sit down.

My mate Pat and I met at the pub before the gig. I have known Pat for 28 years, and we have been to a great many pubs, staring at each other.

'Let's go outside and look at the buses,' said Pat, after a while.

The pub was ideally situated for bus-watching. Its pavement tables boast sweeping views across three bus stops. Pat and I had an absorbing conversation about the longest and shortest bus routes in the city, and we had almost reached a consensus when we met some other friends, who bought some more drinks.

We arrived at the club late, so all the tables were taken. I had to gulp down several beers very quickly, in order to relieve the pressure on my feet. The gig was enlivened, as always, by Earle's magnificent six-strand comb-over. No one would ever know the great man was bald, unless perhaps they were flying over him and mistook his head for a disused radome at the Pine Gap spy station.

The next day, I performed the usual morning-after inventory. I was in the right apartment, sleeping with the right person, I still had the same number of tattoos and the same number of teeth. I was not dressed as a wildebeest. However, I had lost my powers of reason.

I went to the supermarket to buy a breakfast bottle of Vanilla Diet Coke, but I gave the checkout girl the Coke instead of the money, and lolled vacantly in front of her while she tried to figure out what I wanted and I struggled to recall what I had done wrong.

I could not construct a sentence — although I was enthusiastic about making conversation — or walk on the pavement without bumping into people. I realised I was still drunk, and it was all because I had been forced to stand up.

At midday, the hangover hit me, like a particularly interesting bus. My temperature rose monstrously, and I was forced to seek shelter in a bottle shop. I couldn't find my beer in the display fridges in the main part of the shop, so I went searching in the cold room — with the door closed behind me. Ah, it was fantastic, like running out of a sauna and jumping into an icy plunge pool, only to find the pool unaccountably stocked with every beer in the world.

I never wanted to leave the cold room, and wondered how long I could survive there. Beer is a rich source of nutrients: a glass contains more than five per cent of the recommended daily intake of B2, one of only two vitamins that is also a Banana in Pyjamas. And I was surrounded by boxes of wine, made from grapes, which are a well-known source of vitamin C. On the other hand, I quickly had to admit it was getting a bit nippy.

I died a thousand tiny deaths that day, and made a dozen resolutions, all of which were broken within the week.

I still believe live music is a marvellous thing — on a par with other great human inventions such as contraception, refrigeration and Vanilla Diet Coke — but these days I'd prefer it if the bands came to my house. When a man starts to think like that, he knows he's growing old.

opera

noun, 1. highly unpopular form of entertainment

A realistic price for a seat at the opera would probably be about $600. This is due to the enormous expense of flying an entire cast of butter monsters from Rome to Sydney, in a specially adapted Beluga jet, where they are served a five-course meal every hour and each have two chairs to themselves.

The actual cost of a ticket to the Sydney Opera House — the only venue in Australia licensed to stage operas — is probably about $250. The government pays the gap. That means every **CEO** who buys a seat at *La Traviata*, in the attempt to impress a client who would rather be at the football, is subsidised $350 by a sandwich hand or factory worker. The government is reportedly looking at cutting out the middleman, and allowing CEOs to sit directly on working-class people.

passion

***noun*, 1.** warm, wet feeling generated in bastards when they are in the proximity of something that could not possibly be arousing

In the last few years, bastards have suddenly become 'passionate' about their jobs, and even their hobbies. They get hot flushes when they even think about another day in an **HR** workshop, and male bastards go hard at the very mention of a **PowerPoint presentation**.

At time of writing, Microsoft's slogan was 'Your potential. Our passion'. My potential? Really? That is very charitable, because I could not give a toss what happens to Microsoft.

Meanwhile, a new publication called *Redmond Developer News* claims to be 'passionate about Microsoft'. At Lincoln University, Missouri, the Department of Education hopes to train teachers who are 'passionate about students', which is illegal in Australia. Accountants Grant Thornton claim 'a passion for the business of accounting'; there are stranger passions ('plushies', for example, are sexually attracted to soft toys) but none more boring.

In order to get a job or land a contract, bastards will claim to be passionate about anything from the Dewey Decimal Classification System to silicone carbide sandpaper.

On the other hand, no bastard ever says, 'I am passionate about taking it up the arse from my boss.' But they all are.

patch

***noun*, 1. fridge magnet** for a backpack

people persons

***noun*, 1.** bastards bastards

Most bastards pride themselves on being people people, because they have no other skills. A people person is able to get on with people from all walks of life, and is the kind of person who says 'walks of life', as if they all had a particular gait. People people mimic the attitudes and accents of real people, in the hope that other people will like them. They have been monitoring our broadcasts for years, in order to figure out how best to fit in with human society.

Normal people can spot people people by the width of their smile, the strength of their handshake and the frequency with which they employ **air punctuation**. People people are usually eager to start conversations about things that do not interest them — ie the **cricket** — in the belief that they might interest you. They are particularly fond of talking about sport. They do not care what you say, but they consider it important to get you talking. They have seen people having conversations on TV, and they know what it looks like from the outside. Once they have 'established a relationship', they try to sell you something: whether it be Amway, a pay-cut, or the idea of sex with them.

I am not a people person person. The best way to deal with people people is to openly dislike them. This shows them that their heinous scheme has failed, and they may as well pack their electroculturageogscope in their four-dimensional bag and return home to the planet Zog.

The only types worse than people people are dog people and cat people (as distinct from dog- and cat-owners, who tend to be rather nice).

performance review

noun, **1.** con trick; performance

At the end of every financial year, most **managers** are keen for their staff members to have a performance review. Many workers — particularly the younger, less experienced ones — confuse this with a 'pay review', a quaint old custom that no longer exists. Whereas you had some chance of leaving a pay review with the commitment to a pay rise, the most you take from a performance review is nothing whatsoever. The least is considerably less than that.

US HR consultant Harold L. Markle has admitted companies run performance reviews 'to protect themselves against their own employees'. Performance reviews 'put a piece of paper between you and employees, so if you ever have a confrontation, you can go to the file and say, "Here, I've documented this problem."'

When I was still in a position where I had to have meetings with people, I attended a **human resources** meeting about performance reviews. It was the first time they had been tried in the company, and nobody knew what they were for. I was on deadline for my magazine, and could think of many more useful things to discuss than a new process, particularly bearing in mind that most corporate processes have a life only moments longer than the meeting that introduces them.

The performance review procedure was explained using the least comprehensible, most evasive language possible. It was impossible to understand what it was all for. Every employee was to be assessed on a series of criteria, most of which were irrelevant to journalists — such as how long it took them to answer the phone. Journalists do not sit and let the phone ring, they spend all day calling other people and praying they will phone back. HR managers, however, switch their telephones to voice mail, or have their personal assistant tell callers they are 'in a **meeting**'.

I asked how often I was supposed to run these performance reviews, and was told I could do them as often as I wanted — every week, if I felt like it. This was when I realised that HR people were from another world — probably the planet Zog — where work was not something that had to be done but something that existed purely to be measured.

I had about 16 staff. The performance reviews took about an hour to complete. If I allowed myself a bit of administration time to check them through, file them and so on, they would take up half of my working week.

I went back to my office, put the forms in my desk, and never took them out of the drawer. Nobody ever asked me for them, and HR stumbled comically to its next futile project: the Myers-Briggs Type Indicator personality test, or something.

More recently, Stephen Trew, an employment law specialist at Holding Redlich in Sydney, told the *Sydney Morning Herald* that when a client wanted to sack someone, he always advised them that 'a detailed, documented performance review process makes very good evidence'.

So go ahead. Fill out HR's friendly form. What harm can it do?

politicians, irresponsibly named

noun, **1. Downer**s, Stoners and smokers

I am a bit of an Al Gore-sceptic, in that I don't necessarily believe Al Gore exists and, if he does, I'm not sure he is a manmade phenomenon. He may just occur naturally every few years, at around the time of the US presidential elections.

But it would be a disaster if Al Gore were to become president of the greatest country in Iraq. There is enough violence and bloodshed in the world today without a penguin with a head like a clothes peg going around calling himself 'President Gore'. It would be a throwback to the bad old days when people thought a suitable ruler might be somebody named Vlad the Impaler or Ivan the Terrible.

Perhaps, though, some Americans will think it is time they had a president with a scary name because they need him to lead wars on terror (aka laptops) and drugs (aka knees) and other things that do not have armies. If so, our own politicians should take a moment to rethink their own names, and the mixed messages they send out to vulnerable young people.

As is so often the case in this book, the conga line of shame is led by **Alexander Downer**. Surely, with emo kids committing suicide all over the place, and barbiturate use rampant in our suburbs, it is highly irresponsible for our foreigner-mincer to have a name that virtually advertises depressant drugs. Like all generic downers, he lessens the function of a specific part of the body (in this case, the body politic) and is open to abuse (principally by me). But what kind of signal are we giving out to our friends in the international community by having a downer as our representative? Surely we should strive instead to find somebody who is 'high on life'?

One candidate for the job would definitely not be the leader of the NSW National Party, who shamelessly styles himself Andrew Stoner. As Opposition spokesman for education, Andrew has taken on the vital task of rooting out left-wingedness from primary-school textbooks. Yes, this man is going into our schools, peddling his filthy wares. He must be stopped now, before it is too late, and all the little communists in kindy melt their buckets and spades into coke spoons and bongs.

It is indicative of the low priority the Federal Government puts on Aboriginal health that the minister for indigenous affairs is permitted to call himself 'Mal Brough'. It stinks of under-the-table tobacco-company sponsorship, and deals brokered in smoky rooms. Of course, the Mal Brough Man insists his surname is pronounced 'Bruff', which is closer to 'Broth' (as in a hearty, winter soup), but then **Kim Beazley**'s wife, Susie Annus, always emphasised her hard 'a' — and we all know what they called her at school.

A more suitable person to look after indigenous interests would be Joe Hockey, the federal minister for fat, whose name suggests the healthy interest in team sport that his body belies.

In Thailand, boxers often change their names to reflect their sponsors, which is why a recent super-featherweight champion was known as Yodsanan 3K Battery, but was not related to other fighters such as Medgoen 3K Battery or Fahsan 3K Battery.

Perhaps the greatest ever 3K Battery, former junior bantamweight champion Samson 3K Battery eventually changed his name to Samson Toyota-Thailand (he had also been called Samson Dutch Boy Gym for a while).

Perhaps our politicians should follow Samson's example and be obliged to take on the names of the people in whose interests they act. Anti-abortion Health Minister Tony Abbott could, quite legitimately, continue to call himself Tony Abbott (allowing for the misspelling, of course). But Workplace Relations Minister Joe Hockey would become Joe Business Council of Australia; Treasurer Peter Costello would become Peter BRW Rich List; and John Howard would, at last, become John President of the United States of America.

Post-it note

noun, **1. fridge magnet** for a computer screen, telephone, document, shoe

In the days before Post-its, we used to make notes in the margins of memos. This had the drawback of defacing documents, but the invaluable benefit that the annotation remained where it was.

Post-it notes, or 'yellow stickies', were invented by a scientist named Art Fry in 1980, for reasons best known to himself. On first glance, they would appear, like **HR consultants**, to have no useful application, but in fact you can stick them anywhere to remind you of anything. You can attach them to your stuff or to other people's stuff, to animate or inanimate objects. It does not matter too much, because whatever you attach them to they will quickly become unstuck from, and gather together in small piles elsewhere.

Post-its stick to each other, and they stick to anything that goes past. At any given moment in any office anywhere in the world, there is at least one person walking around with a note that says 'Hamish called while u were @ lunch' attached to the sole of their shoe.

Post-it notes have been recruited into the corporate world's so-called 'war on information', in which bastards continually attempt to blur the line between news and advertising using sinister tools such as **advertorial** and **Alan Jones**. Fairfax newspapers regularly appear with stupid yellow stickies on the front page, paid for by advertisers, reminding the readers of things that are of no interest to them, such as the possibility of buying a discounted Hewlett-Packard printer when they purchase a full-price HP computer.

Art Fry has said, 'When Post-its are still used after I am gone, it will be as if a part of me will live on forever.' In this, he is mistaken. After he is gone, it will be as if he is dead, just like everybody else, except somebody will have left a yellow sticky on the lid of his coffin saying, 'Do not open' or 'Hamish called while u were @ lunch'.

PowerPoint presentation

noun, **1.** the blindingly obvious reduced to point form

A particularly absorbing type of **meeting** where the keynote speaker is a laptop computer.

private school

noun, **1.** public school

Private schools in Australia are Federal Government-funded schools for the children of rich people. Public schools in Australia are Federal Government-funded schools for the children of everyone else. Greater Public Schools are so-called because they attract a greater amount of Federal Government funding. This is not a joke. This is not satire. This is true.

Rich parents make a contribution to the cost of the schooling of their children, in the form of 'school fees', but these do not pay the full price of the lush, green 'level playing fields' we hear so much about, or the state-of-the-art science labs, enthusiastic school bullies etc. The Federal Government steps in to fill the gap, with taxes paid by poorer people, and leaves the balance of public-school funding to the states.

Although about two-thirds of Australian children attend public schools, more than two-thirds of Federal Government education funding goes to subsidising private schools. The more wealthy the school, the more Federal Government money it gets. As the great — although, sadly, bearded — economics writer Ross Gittins has pointed out, 'Australia is the only country where the provision of public funding for private schools is the dominant function of the national government – and constitutes the largest item in its education budget.'[1]

Private schools in Australia are often religiously based. Since most religious beliefs are mutually exclusive, this means at least some of them must teach rubbish. Christian schools teach that Jesus was the Messiah, and he has been and gone, and won't be back until the end of time, so don't bother waiting up for him. Jewish schools teach that the Messiah is on his way, and the prophet Elijah may well turn up at your Passover dinner to usher in the start of the Messianic era, which is why it is best to leave an empty seat for him. Logically, either (a) one of these contentions is true; or (b) neither is true.

It seems odd that atheist, agnostic or Zoroastrian taxpayers should pay for the religious education of well-off Christians or Jews when, in the very best scenario, only one of those faiths teaches the truth, and the other peddles blasphemies, the adoption of which may well result in their pupils being damned for all time. It seems doubly odd that private schools should be allowed to call themselves 'private' when they attract more taxpayers'

---

[1] 'More privilege for the privileged', Ross Gittins, *Sydney Morning Herald*, 23/05/07.

money than state schools. Perhaps you need a taxpayer-subsidised private school education – like **elite**-bashers **Alexander Downer**, **Philip Ruddock** and **Amanda Vanstone** — to understand it.

property developer

noun, **1.** crook

pub, gastro

noun, **1.** a pub for people who don't like drinking beer, teetotallers, restaurant critics etc

Recently, my brother and I were on our way home from the pub when we dropped into his local servo to get some supplies. In the UK, as in most of Europe, beer is sold at garages, so as to facilitate drunk driving and keep the population at a manageable level. My brother picked up eight cans of Foster's, then remembered he had not fed his tropical fish.

'Do you have any fish food?' he asked the Asian woman at the checkout.

'We have tuna sandwiches,' she said.

'But my fish don't eat tuna sandwiches,' said my brother.

'No, nor do mine,' she agreed.

It was an illustration of the ambiguity of the English language, particularly evident when one partner in the conversation is drunk and the other is Chinese. It also shed light on one of the many reasons fish may be reluctant to use petrol stations.

My brother and I had been for a pub meal with my brother's girlfriend, who, by an extraordinary coincidence, is also my ex-wife. I am sad to report that contemporary English pub food is in a sorry state. Until the mid-1990s, many great English meals were only ever found in pubs. Since many pubs went 'gastro' and began to serve dishes with jus, reductions and caramelised everything, real pub food — such as the fisherman's basket, a high-concept dish, based on an imaginative projection of what a fisherman's catch might look like after a nuclear holocaust, when everything in the ocean had become bright orange, crispy and rectangular — has all but died out.

As I have said before, genuine pub food should not aspire beyond a certain level. Just as you don't visit a restaurant to drink draught beer, play bad pool and scrawl lewd graffiti on the condom machine, you don't go into a saloon bar to sample haute cuisine.

There is no point in having 'twice-cooked' chicken on a pub menu. All real pub food is cooked twice: once in the frying pan and once in the microwave.

The flavour of pub food is best kept to a minimum, so as not to interfere with the taste of beer. Dishes should be high in carbohydrates and devoid of nutritional value. In this way, they are best suited to their function of 'soaking up' the beer, a mysterious physiological process whereby alcohol is rendered harmless by hot chips. They also help the drinker to develop the physique necessary to put away a greater quantity of beer in the future.

As it turned out, my brother, his girlfriend and I could not get a table at any of the local gastropubs. Eventually, we managed to find a deservedly unpopular country pub to dine on burger and chips, and it was suitably rubbish.

I was in the Subiaco Hotel in Perth a few months later and it was impossible to buy a burger from the bistro. I could, however, have ordered japanese crumbed tiger prawns, wakami salad, sushi rice and crisp sesame gyzo; chilled blue swimmer crab, orange syrup salad and harissa labna brik pastry; or avocado cous cous tabbouleh, egyptian duck egg, dukkah and fried breads. Each of these descriptions contains at least one word I do not understand, and none includes a capital letter. This is not the kind of confusion a man needs when he is only ordering from the counter because he can't find his way to the local kebab shop.

Gastropubs offer pub-style service in pub-style ambience with pub-style crowds, at restaurant-style prices. In doing so, they attract the wrong crowd. There were 25 tables of diners at the Subi, and only three people were drinking beer. What business do the rest of them have taking up chairs that could be used by people having difficulty standing up?

In my letterbox last year was a flyer inviting me to think of a new name for the pub up the road, asking what food, entertainment and music style I'd prefer to find there, and assuring me my submission would go into a draw to win a 'Mega Lifestyle Hamper'.

The food I would have liked to see in the pub was Pub Food, as brought over from England by the First Publicans on the First

Fleet: steak and chips, steak sandwich and chips, burger and chips and fish and chips. Since it is — quite rightly — illegal to tie up vegetarians and force them to eat proper food, there would have been a vegetarian option on the menu as well. This would have contained all the main food groups eaten by vegetarians and be called 'bowl of chips'.

A meat pie would have been available which, like all meat pies, would unaccountably be described as 'famous', even though I have rarely come across a meat pie that was better known than, for example, a spring roll or a lamppost.

For entertainment, I would have liked to see a jukebox. Not one of these new-fangled video jukeboxes — which, take it from me, will never catch on — but a diner-style model that looks like the front of a car, and is always broken. There would also have been a pinball machine, which would always be broken, and a bar billiards table, which nobody would be certain how to use. In the toilets would have been a condom machine, graffitied with entertaining standards such as 'this chewing gum tastes funny', which would always be empty.

I could do without live music most of the week, but on Sunday afternoons three tremendously bearded Irishmen could have formed a cluster like a hairy shamrock and played *The Leaving of Liverpool* and *The Green Fields of France* with a guitar, fiddle and something that looks like a tambourine but is banged like a drum. And nobody would ever listen to them.

I was a bit stumped when it came to a name. I've never been to a good pub with 'Station' in its title or a bad pub whose sign bore the word 'Exchange', but I'm sure they exist. Stupid pairings such as The Kebab and Calculator and

The Senate and **Santo** are traditional, but The Spring Roll and Lamppost does not have a ring to it, and nor does anything else I could come up with, so I rang the pub to see what the frontrunners were.

So far, said the barman, the suggestion box on the bar had been stuffed mainly by 'drunken people trying to be funny' — 'The Rat Hole' had been mooted.

It might be time to go back to the days when pubs were named for the clientele they hoped to attract. Commercial travellers in every country town knew they were welcome at the Commercial Hotel, for instance, and criteria throughout Australia would always find congenial — if conditional — company in The Criterion. It is a far cry from that situation in contemporary Western Australia, where I recently came across Clancy's Fish Pub, which serves many local microbrews but no actual fish food. This might shed light on one of the many reasons fish rarely drop in for a pint.

pub, Irish

noun, **1.** pub, non-Irish

The first pub I regularly drank in was an Irish pub in England, called the Princess of Wales. I think it was probably named after Catherine of Aragon, although I had never thought about it until five minutes ago. The point is, it was not called 'the Princess of

Ireland' because (a) Ireland does not have a **royal family**; and (b) Irish people did not used to have to be told where to drink. The Princess was filled (insofar as it ever filled) with Irish builders, and on the jukebox was Paddy Reilly's *The Town I Loved So Well*, The Fureys' *Maggie* and mawkish country ballads such as *Crystal Chandelier* that still haunt me today. It was an Irish pub because Irish people frequented it, not an Irish theme park for Friday-night Guinness drinkers.

The Princess of Wales is a curry house now, but it lives on in my heart as a model of how a pub should be: shabby, half-empty and haunted by half-mad Irishmen. It was like drinking in a Pogues song.

When I came to Australia, the closest thing to an English local pub I could find was the Rose and Crown in Paddington, Sydney. It was a classier joint than the Princess of Wales, to be sure, but a public toilet in Paddington (should they ever happen to build one) would be classier than most pubs in the town I loved so well. I liked the Rose and Crown because its customers were people who lived nearby. These days, it's called something like 'Mick MacPaddy Fitzpatrick's Genuoine Oirish Saloon, To Be Sure, Aye, 'Tis So, Begorrah', and it is another infected cell in the international cancer of fake Irish pubs — plastic Paddy palaces that mutate like melanomas in every major city in the developed world. They seem to be assembled from an Ikea-style kit containing a Guinness pump, a hurling stick, a pack of framed adverts for brands of cigarettes and spirits that no longer exist, black-and-white pictures of heavily moustachioed Gaelic football teams and an astonishingly boring poster of pub doors.

A bizarre cast of dead or non-existent Irish people ostensibly owns or runs Irish pubs all over the world. In Australia, Perth is particularly prone to Imaginary Irish Landlord Syndrome, with hotels called Rosie O'Grady's, Paddy Malone's, Paddy Hannan's, J.B. O'Reilly's, Fibber McGee's and Durty Nelly's.

While actual pubs in Ireland are home to all manner of toothless lunatics and some of the world's worst bar meals, fake Irish pubs tend to be pick-up joints packed with parasites from every unproductive corner of corporate culture, all trying to have sex with each other's personal assistants. At least the food is more appetising than the real thing, although its connections with anything Irish are often dragged beyond the limits of credulity and tend to run along the lines of Paddy's Traditional Galway-style Burger, a minced beef patty in a sesame seed bun, served with shamrock-green lettuce.

There is a large pub in Canberra called King O'Malley's. This is a good name for an Irish pub because (a) King O'Malley actually existed; (b) he was not Irish; (c) he was the politician who banned alcohol from the city from 1910 to 1928. Therefore, King O'Malley was the last person anyone might bump into at King O'Malley's, although, to be fair, the Princess of Wales rarely turned up at the Princess of Wales either.

public relations

noun, **1.** journalism with the truth taken out

A pioneer of modern corporate PR was Mohammed Saeed al-Sahaf, information minister in Saddam Hussein's government until 2003, when the Iraqi regime was overthrown by a broad global coalition of the US Army, the British Army, two Australians and a former metalworker from Wroclaw in Poland. Unkindly nicknamed 'Comical Ali' — after 'Chemical Ali', who ordered a chemical-weapons attack on the Kurds — and 'the Minister for Silly Talks', Mohammed regularly declared that the Coalition was suffering massive losses, and its troops about to 'commit suicide on the walls of Baghdad', as they went from virtually unopposed victory to virtually unopposed victory.

'The soldiers of Saddam Hussein have given them a lesson they will never forget,' he said, even though the soldiers of Saddam Hussein had vanished. He predicted the Americans 'are going to surrender or be burned in their tanks'. This sounded funnier in April 2003 than it does now.

In one of his final pronouncements as information minister, he stood on the roof of the Palestine Hotel and told reporters, 'I triple guarantee you, there are no American soldiers in Baghdad,' when US tanks could be seen a couple of hundred metres away.

When Mohammed was interviewed after the war had (apparently) ended, he adopted the classic bastard defence that he was a 'professional'. He had no sense of humour, and cited 'authentic sources — many sources' as the basis of his information.

You need know no more about the average 'practitioner' of PR than the story of Corporate Ali.

public transport, abuse of disabled seats on

noun, **1.** common practice among lunchtime drunks, schizophrenic fascists etc

Mad people and drunks please note, the first seat on most public buses is reserved for people with a physical disability. Although mental illness is as debilitating as any physical infirmity, it is not the type of ill health that requires its sufferer to accept a seat before everyone else on the bus. Try to think of it like this: deafness is a disability, but deaf people are not allowed to park their car in parking spots reserved for the disabled.

Equally, although drunks find it harder to stand than sober people, and high levels of alcohol can cause the imbiber to mimic many of the symptoms of both mental and physical illness, if you are feeling *that* unstable you should not be on the bus, because you are probably going to throw up.

Abusers of disabled seating should not despair, however. In Sydney, at least, there *are* special seats on the bus, set aside just for you. These are the two seats on either side of the aisle that face the rest of the passengers. These provide the insane with the delusion-affirming sensation of continually moving in a different direction to everyone else, and also offer the perfect platform from which to lecture a captive audience about freemasonry, barcodes and the coming Time of the Beast.

This seating also has a predictable effect on members of other vulnerable sectors of society. Drunks may like to take the opportunity to say a few words about their ex–wife, or offer solutions to a range of social problems supposedly heightened by immigration. Old ladies may be gripped by an urge to point out where department stores used to be, and enlighten younger people about how much various provisions used to cost.

purple cow

noun, **1.** non-existent animal used to illustrate non-existent concepts, eg originality in marketing

Bastards love their imaginary menagerie. If they are not preoccupied with finding the **invisible elephant**, they are often out looking for a purple cow.

Small children like to be taught about the world through the exploits of talking ducks and the like. In the same way, executives — who are generally not big readers — require short, pithy stories about their favourite animals to understand the world around them. Certain **brand** managers have been known to cry themselves to sleep if they do not hear the story about the purple cow.

The concept of the purple cow came from **marketing guru** Seth Godin, who had an epiphany while driving through the French countryside — possibly the most beautiful landscape in the world. Although he was at first 'enchanted' by all the French cows in the fields, he soon realised they were 'boring'. 'A purple cow, though: Now, that would really stand out,' he wrote, apparently seriously.

Therefore, a business that was different, and which would command the attention of the market, would be a purple cow. In all but biology. And logic.

In the long run, a purple cow has little chance of survival. The fact of being purple conveys no evolutionary advantages for a cow and would probably lead to other cows failing to recognise her as one of their own. Bulls would not breed with her, farmers would not milk her for fear of getting eggplant-flavoured thickshakes, and children would throw stones at her from behind barbed-wire fences.

Queen

proper noun, 1. rock band popular with several generations of bastards

Why is it okay to like Queen again? Was there some kind of truth commission that absolved them of responsibility for playing at the South African tourist resort Sun City during the Apartheid era? Was there a critical re-evaluation of *Fat Bottomed Girls* one night when I was out at the pub? Is it all because of bloody *Wayne's World*?[1]

How could the formerly right-on, formerly funny comedian Ben Elton have written a musical about a band that, in the mid-

---

[1] Probably, yes.

1980s, broke the African National Congress's embargo on artists performing in South Africa, even though its singer Freddie Mercury was himself an African Indian?

The band said they were just apolitical entertainers (yawn) playing where the crowds wanted to see them. But in the wake of the bad publicity that surrounded their decision to offer a soft endorsement to the Apartheid regime, they grew a social conscience and appeared on the first Live Aid show. Sales of their old records soared.

Queen were suddenly the friends of black people and, if Freddie had lived long enough to write his autobiography, he would no doubt have contrived to include a photograph of himself with Nelson Mandela. (Watch out for a similar picture in John Howard's political memoirs, even though John firmly opposed sanctions against Pretoria.)

As a band, Queen managed to fuse the high pomp of opera with the low pomp of heavy metal, a task just as valuable as the fusion of, for example, strawberries and mackerel, or bacon and a car, and just as artistically successful.

I have always, um, quite liked their early single *Seven Seas Of Rye*, though.

racist but... person who is not a

noun, **1.** a racist

Nobody ever said, 'I am not a racist but I believe there is no scientific basis to conclude the behaviour of a given group of people is determined by certain shared genetic characteristics.' They are more likely to say, 'I am not a racist but have you ever wondered why there are no great Aboriginal chess players?' In the interests of clarity, people tempted to prefix a comment with the rider, 'I'm not a racist but...' should simply substitute for it, 'I am a racist and...'

regulations, dress

noun, 1. by-laws to ensure crims are not kept waiting outside nightclubs

Melbourne's gangsters smartened up for their last gang war, in which more than 25 men have been murdered in six years. When an investigating cop blamed 'television' for the gangsters' behaviour, he was surely talking about *The Sopranos*, and he was surely not suggesting that an over-identification with the show had caused several dozen grown-up drug-dealers to start, er, whacking each other.

What they took from *The Sopranos* was The Look. Photographed outside the Coroner's Court after the death of their latest nephew, they all look like *the* nephew, Christopher Moltisanti, in dark Italian suits draped over tight, black, v-neck knits.

They are serious people. They kill each other. But they would have no trouble gaining admittance to any nightclub in Australia, even if they did not shoot their way in.

The tradition of tradesmen adopting distinguishing styles of dress dates back to the European craft guilds of the Middle Ages. For gangsters, it is particularly useful, as it allows them to recognise each other, and thus ensures they shoot the right people.

Other special-interest groups have evolved their own unique costumes, as a shorthand means of identification. A tall, skinny guy wearing silver jewellery, a Slipknot T-shirt and a black leather jacket indoors is probably saying, 'I am the new IT geek.' A man wearing a polyester shirt and grey flannel trousers with white sandshoes is clearly proclaiming, 'I am a born-again Christian,' just as a bloke with his shirt tucked into his shorts is unmistakably announcing, 'I am a child molester.'

For leisurewear, crims tend to favour adidas shell suits, the standard uniform of junkies and much of the suburban working class. For this reason, the wrong people do sometimes get shot. It is unclear why Australian heroin addicts have so wholeheartedly embraced sportswear, since they are the last people to take any exercise. Once again, however, it serves to make them known to the wider community, and explain why the person sitting next to you has fallen asleep dribbling on the bus.

The dress regulations in RSLs seem designed to exclude a type of troublemaker who doesn't exist. Exactly who wears a hat, a singlet, stubbies and thongs, and lives in the city? They might as well put up a big sign saying, 'Crocodile Dundee Not Welcome Here (after 7pm).'

Bouncers in Sydney and Melbourne spend much of their time trying to keep badly dressed people out of clubs. As a harm-minimisation strategy, this is wildly misguided. Unfashionable-looking people don't start fights. They don't have the confidence. All the aggro comes from the sharp kids with the buzz-cuts, the soft leather jackets and the rap-star jewellery, the mirror-polished shoes and incurious eyes.

Bouncers should know this, because they look like that themselves.

There used to be a strip joint on the Gold Coast called Players Showgirls. The sign banned all the usual iconic Aussie gear, including thongs — even though the number of fights started by blokes wearing thongs could be counted on the bruised toes of one foot — and a few more locally specific problem garments such as bikie colours. It even said: 'No gang names'. What could that mean? Would they refuse you entrance if you're called 'Scarface'?

I drank six bottles of beer then phoned them to find out.

Cindy: 'Hello, Showgirls, this is Cindy.'

Me: Hi. Would I have to book a table if a *gang* of us comes in after midnight?

Cindy: 'Um, no, not a problem. Just come up to the door.'

Me: It doesn't matter how many of us there are?

Cindy: 'Er, no. How many are there?'

Me: Me, Knuckles, Skull, the Guvnor... about ten.

Cindy: 'Yeah, sure. Not a problem. We'll see you there.'

Northern Territorians pride themselves in not having as many rules as the rest of us. Cyclists don't have to wear helmets, X-rated videos are sold legally, and remote roads have no speed limits. The pubs, however, have more dress regulations than the Royal Australian Navy. The Blue Heeler in Darwin is fairly typical. It permits no work clothes and no singlets after 7pm — 'no excuses': 'No shoes, no shirt, no shorts, no service'.

That's not 'no shorts' as in you can't wear shorts; it's 'no shorts' as in 'you will not be served if you come in without trousers'. It is high time the rest of Australia adopted this policy. I have lost count of the number of occasions I have been sitting in a pub in Sydney, Melbourne or Perth, and suddenly noticed the bloke on the next table has come out in his underpants.

Perhaps it is a particular problem in the Blue Heeler because everybody in work trousers takes them off at 7pm, so as not to be caught out under rule number one.

ringtone, polyphonic

noun, 1. fridge magnet for a mobile phone

royal family, British

proper noun, 1. a German royal family

I have never met the late Princess Diana, although my ex-wife once showed her how to put a condom on a banana, during a pay TV show about sexual health. From a distance, it seemed to me Diana lived her life like a candle in the wind, never knowing who to turn to when the rain set in, except James Gilbey, James Hewitt, Barry Mannakee, David Waterhouse, Oliver Hoare, Dr Hasnat Khan, Bryan Adams and Dodi Al Fayed.

After a brief period of marriage to a man who wanted to be a tampon, Diana was murdered by MI6, the paparazzi and her drunken chauffeur, when a plot to fake her death went wrong. The real target was Dodi Al Fayed, a metre-high flightless bird that is related to the Egyptian owner of Harrods.

If Diana had lived — which she did, because she and Dodi survive together secretly on a desert island (probably Mauritius, where Dodi was once endemic) — she would have become gradually less famous. As her profile fell, she would almost certainly have appeared in the UK version of *Celebrity Big Brother*, and been voted out because she was 'too posh'. A pirate video of Diana having sex with love-rat James Hewitt would suddenly and mysteriously become widely available (although this would have nothing to do with the love-rat himself) and many people would download it to their cell phones. She would earn extra money by releasing cover versions of Elton John songs, and sing *Goodbye Reginald Kenneth Dwight* at Elton's state funeral.

Diana's husband, to his chagrin, was not a sanitary product but a member of the British royal family, who changed their name from the House of Saxe-Coburg and Gotha to the House of Windsor, so that nobody would notice they were German. The British royal family is known to do a 'great job'. The Queen, in particular, is very good at wearing a crown and sitting on a throne. Charles, her eldest son, would like to acquire these skills too, over his mother's dead body. Since his grandma, the presciently named 'Queen Mother', lived to 101, he may be forced to confine himself to interesting pronouncements about architecture, the environment and alternative medicine. This will still be a life well lived, and he can always console himself with the fact that he was married to one of the most beautiful women in the world, Camilla Parker Bowles, an expensive type of gargoyle.

During a phone call to Camilla, recorded while he was still married to Diana, Charles told his lover he would like to live inside her trousers. 'I want to be reincarnated as your tampon,' he said, displaying his twin enthusiasms for unconventional spiritual beliefs and feminine hygiene products. Although Charles's fantasy was not **brand** specific, it is believed his prominent ears would have made him most suitable for use as a 'winged sanitary pad'.

The British royal family is also the Australian royal family, thank God. I would not have moved to Australia if I'd had to change royal families. All this fashionable talk of republicanism is basket-weaving, unpatriotic, **black-armband** nonsense, and an insult to the diggers who fought two world wars so that Australia could have a German royal family.

ruddock

verb, **1.** to ruddock: to arbitrarily redefine one's perimeters, in such a way as to make something somebody else's problem. Eg 'She ruddocked her herbaceous borders into next door's garden, so Mrs Nauruvianname would have to water her plants'

I once saw Attorney-General Philip Maxwell Ruddock at the airport, and I was fascinated by the way he manages to simultaneously resemble both an undertaker and a recently reanimated corpse.

The sighting confirmed my suspicions that the Philip who had joined Amnesty International had died — perhaps after being thrown off a sinking ship by his parents — and his bloated body had been drained of blood and water and put into the service of an evil scheme masterminded by his political enemies.

The real Philip appears to have perished in a certain maritime incident in the early 1990s. Until that time, Philip, who once crossed the floor to support a Labor measure to guarantee Australian immigration policy did not discriminate on racial grounds, was a reasonable man, although he still looked a bit like that scarecrow thing that used to appear in the opening credits of the early, black-and-white episodes of *Star Trek*.

Like **Alexander Downer**, Philip had to fight tooth and nail to get where he is today. Philip Maxwell Ruddock is the son of Maxwell Ruddock, a lowly member of State Parliament. But the young Philip had one thing his father did not: the name Philip.

He battled his way through Sydney's notoriously rough Barker College, and joined Federal Parliament in 1973.

As Minister for Immigration, Philip was the first person to announce the refugees on board the *SIEV 4* had thrown their children overboard, when they had not. In 2001, he introduced the Border Protection Bill, which put Christmas Island out of Australia and Nauru in it.

With friends like Philip Maxwell Ruddock, refugees do not need enemies like Philip Maxwell Ruddock.

S

same page

noun, **1.** a place bastards would like everyone to assemble; a Mecca for bastards

Bastards become agitated and fidgety if they are not on the same page as everyone else. This is a fate as bad as being outside the **loop**, or having one's thinking inside the box.

It can be difficult to remain on the same page as a bastard, because they read slowly — except Jeffrey Archer's books, which they 'can't put down' — and keep pace with their lips.

Bastard-busting tip number six: When a bastard asks, 'Are we on the same page?' pick up a telephone book, open it at your name, and slam it closed around their head.

(This works best if your surname falls towards the middle of the alphabet and you live in a metropolitan area with a substantial *White Pages*. If you are called Xerxes Xylophone and have a house in Tasmania, you may wish to reconsider your position. If you are on your local sex offenders' register, you could offer to have the bastard's name included alongside your own, although if you are on the sex offenders' register you are probably a bastard yourself.)

Santo Santoro

proper noun, **1.** Bastard Bastardo

Last year, I had the flu but, despite my illness, I was able to fly to a journalism awards ceremony in Queensland. I have a long history of coming runner-up in competitions. I won't bother you with a list of my humiliations. Suffice to say, I was judged the second-best IT investigative journalist in the country in 1998.

In Brisbane, I was up for a prize for positive portrayal of old people, based on a feature I wrote suggesting Rolf Harris might still be able to pull chicks by singing *Tie Me Kangaroo Down, Sport*. The honours in my section were presented by Senator Santo Santoro, then Federal Minister for Ageing, who delivered an intelligent, moving, Churchillian speech, attacking Australian journalistic standards to a room full of Australian journalists. He even made a funny joke about the old adage that the only truth in newspapers is in the ad pages. Ha ha ha. Ha ha ha. Ha ha ha. Now fuck off.

Santo was one of those Liberal 'members' who saw his prime parliamentary role as protecting society from the ABC (the broadcaster, not the alphabet). It must have been gratifying for him to see the ABC receive so many nominations in the awards.

The most endearing thing about these middle-class, chardonnay-drinking, latte-sipping, cheese-eating, soon-to-announce-surrender-in-Iraq monkeys is their engorged sense of victimhood. They have been in government since 1996. They have a majority in both houses. In Federal elections, they consistently win the endorsement of the overwhelming majority of the print media. They themselves publish millions of dollars' worth of taxpayer-funded propaganda for their union-bashing, indirect-taxing, refugee-demonising agenda. They have even branch-stacked the board of the ABC. But they still behave like an embattled minority, fighting for their right to a fair hearing; or bold contrarians, valiantly swimming against the stream of *bien-pensant* conformity. The longer he talked, the more I realised I could not shake Santo's hand when I won the award. What if some of his DNA rubbed off? I thought maybe I should punch him instead. It was a tough choice to make, but, luckily, I did not have to.

I came second, as always.

However, you piss me off and you're dead meat. It soon turned out that the only truth in Santo's declaration of assets to parliament was in the omissions.

Nobody elected Santo to the Senate. He was selected in 2002 to replace a Liberal member who had resigned. He had lost his safe Queensland Liberal seat in the state election in 2001, when he was defeated by child killer Bella Albrecht from *Prisoner*.

Now Santo will never face the polls, because he has resigned in the face of a scandal about his professional integrity. Now, I'm not one to gloat. Oh, sorry, yes I am. I must have got myself mixed up with the Dalai Lama.

Like many other battlers, Santo could not always keep track of his share-holdings. Any busy person could have forgotten they held a financial interest in a biotech company, especially as, in Santo's case, the purchase was 'handled by a person other than [his] regular investment advisers'.

Nobody could have been more surprised than Santo when he discovered that he had made a $6000 profit selling shares that had cost him $6000. As soon as he realised what he had done, Santo gave the profit to charity.

The charity he chose was the Family Council of Queensland, which was (a) not a registered charity, and (b) the body whose president had advised him to buy the shares in the first place.

It soon transpired that Santo had forgotten to disclose his financial interests in a total of 72 companies.

While a lesser man might have found himself so busy buying and selling shares, and then forgetting about them, that he would not have had time to scrutinise the financial affairs of others, public-spirited Santo, whose family investments are so vast that he had to hire an auditor to 'scour' them, managed to make the time to speak at the Young Liberals Conference in January 2007. There, the anosognosic Santo described Australian trade unionism as a protection racket that funded the 'lavish lifestyles of the industrial elite'.

Eventually, in the face of massive evidence against him, Santo did the only honourable thing: he blamed the media.

He retired from the Senate. 'My continued presence here presents an excuse for the double standards to be played out in the nation's papers on a daily basis,' he said, ripe with contrition for deceiving Parliament.

Now that Santo is not busy representing people who did not vote for him, he might find more time for his own journalistic venture. *The Conservative*, the 'quarterly' magazine founded by Santo in September 2005, has only managed to squeeze out two issues, the last in 2006. Reading through the debut issue, which includes an essay by Santo himself, there are times when I think there might be some accuracy in the adage that the only truth in the magazine is found in the advertisements. Of which there are none.

Saudi Arabia

proper noun, **1.** Saudi America

Saudi Arabia is an unflinching ally of the US in the **War on Terror** (or WOT). This is a good job, since the war was started by Osama bin Laden, who is a Saudi, and the September 11 hijackers, 15 of whom were Saudis.

In retaliation for attacks on American interests by Saudi Arabians, the US invaded Iraq.

In retaliation for attacks on Australian tourists by Indonesian terrorists in Bali, Australia invaded Iraq, too. In retaliation for the fact it never wanted to be in the Eastern Bloc, Poland also invaded Iraq. Saudi Arabia did not invade Iraq, despite the fact Iraq is next door to Saudi Arabia, whereas Australia is 13,395 kilometres away.

There are no churches or synagogues in Saudi Arabia, because it is illegal to practise Christianity or Judaism in Saudi Arabia (Jews are not even entitled to enter the country), unlike in Saddam Hussein's Iraq. When US troops were stationed in Saudi Arabia, to protect the kingdom from Saddam Hussein's Iraq, they were not officially permitted to celebrate Christmas or to drink beer. (It is now effectively illegal to drink beer in some parts of Iraq that are under Sharia law, although it was not under Saddam Hussein.)

Saudi Arabia is officially **teetotal**. It combined its twin roles as the world's bastion of militant teetotalism and an unflinching warrior against terror when a British expatriate worker living in Riyadh, Saudi Arabia, Christopher Rodway, was killed by a car bomb in 2000. The Saudis, who were at the time pretending to believe there was no terrorism in their country, pretended to believe that Christopher was a casualty in a turf war between bootleggers, and that he had been killed by his friends, Sandy Mitchell, Bill Sampson and Leslie Walker, because they all drank at the Celtic Corner, an unofficial pub run by Sandy and Les. Sandy was chief anaesthetic technician at the Security Forces Hospital in Riyadh, where he worked saving Saudi lives. Under the authority of Prince Naif bin Abdul Aziz, Sandy was chained up, tortured all night, punched, kicked, spat on and hit with sticks. The Saudis beat the soles of his feet with an axe handle until he admitted to blowing up

Christopher. Sandy later said, 'I would have confessed to anything to stop the pain.'

The two men were sentenced to death *by crucifixion*.

So the brave drinkers of Saudi Arabia were arrested, tortured and almost executed for the crime of being targeted by Islamic terrorists. They were released after nine al-Qaeda suicide bombers killed 35 people and injured 200 in an attack on an expat compound in Riyadh in May 2003. But five Saudis were transferred from Guantanamo Bay two days after the attack, apparently in exchange for the British drinkers.

Eighteen months after Saudi Arabians attacked the US, the coalition of the willing invaded Iraq because Saddam was an evil dictator who murdered his own people. Only six months after Saudi Arabians attacked the US, there was a fire at a school in Mecca. Schoolgirls fleeing the flames were beaten and pushed back into the fire by the Saudi religious police, the Commission for the Promotion of Virtue and Prevention of Vice, because they were not wearing veils. According to the BBC, at least 14 girls died. This is not the same as murdering your own people, because Saudi Arabia is our unflinching ally in the War on Terror.

security guard

noun, **1.** fish minder

I used to live across the road from the Fish Markets in Pyrmont,

Sydney, in the days when there was a security guard who stood opposite one of the larger fishmongers, his pistol hanging at his waist. I always wanted to ask him what were his rules of engagement. Would he shoot me for stealing a red emperor, for example, or a nice piece of blue-eye? Was fish theft much of a problem, anyway? How come he was allowed to carry a gun to protect fish, whereas I couldn't pack a pistol in case I was attacked by an armed security guard gone postal? Would he give his life for a mackerel? How is it that you can hire gunmen to guard your bream, but not yourself? Why is perch more important than people?

But I never even spoke to the bloke, and one day he disappeared, the threat to fish having presumably dissipated to the extent that his services were no longer required.

Static security guards tend to come from the same recruitment pool as criminals, since security is only an attractive career choice if you've got no qualifications or experience and have perhaps been out of the workforce for several years: if you have spent much of your life in prison, for instance.

When Sydney had a problem with bastards harassing young women on trains, CityRail hired more security staff, who proceeded to harass young women on trains. One quizzed a 15-year-old girl on how she had lost her virginity and which sexual positions she enjoyed. Two other star recruits were brothers from Pakistan, who went on to become notorious gang rapists.

In 2003, 292 security guards across NSW had their licences revoked after they were convicted of serious crimes.

So, if you want to know the time, ask a security guard. He has probably done some, after all.

The idea of giving special training to private security guards so they could help protect the 2007 Asia-Pacific Economic Co-operation summit in Sydney from terrorism was quickly shelved.

'We looked at it but the industry here is rife with organised crime, Middle Eastern crime gangs and bikies,' said a 'police source'. 'It was too much of a risk.'[1]

Despite their apparent links with 'Middle Eastern crime gangs', security guards have been given a key role to play in the **War on Terror**, which has developed into a war on people who take their laptops onto planes. It is a war fought by security guards, whose weapons include conveyor belts, x-ray machines, and a kind of cattle prod that is supposed to beep if you have recently been in contact with explosives. Travellers used to have to take the battery out of their laptop and put it in a special tray, but after a spate of attacks by terrorists not using dummy laptops with phony batteries, it was decided that they only had to take their laptop out of its case and put it in a special tray. Countless lives have been saved this way.

At Sydney Airport, I shuffled through the security arch to be taken aside by the guy with the explosive-detection sensor. This always happens to me. He found nothing. This always happens, too. I asked how often he got positive results.

About two in five, he replied, unconvincingly.

What? Two in five air passengers are terrorists?

No, he explained. Two in five have recently handled chemicals.

Yeah, right.

---

[1] 'Private guards kept out of APEC equation', Tom Allard, *Sydney Morning Herald*, 11/07/07.

The next guard I asked told me the figure is closer to '0.1 per cent'. It was 'very rare' for anyone to set off his machine. In fact, I suspect nobody ever has.

The lanky spectre of Osama also reared its goggle-eyed head in a shopping arcade in Melbourne's Chinatown. I was taking a picture of a dragon painted on a plaster pillar when a security guard apologetically asked me to put my camera away. Management had banned photography inside the building 'after September 11'. It's a slippery slope from snapping outside a Cantonese restaurant to flying an airliner into the World Trade Center, and I was just grateful the authorities caught me in time.

serial killer

noun, **1.** fucking idiot

Sheik Taj Din al-Hilali

proper noun, **1.** widely misunderstood passionate feminist

Sheik Taj Din al-Hilali was, until June 2007, the mufti of the Islamic community of Australia, among whom he has no support. He shares this distinction with Muslim leaders throughout the world, from Hamas to the Taliban to Saddam Hussein, none of whom had any support among the Muslims who elected them, fought for them, or looked to them for leadership (by contrast, it is equally well known that all Jewish people the world over support every government of Israel, even if they did not vote for it, would not fight for it and, in fact, support the opposition).

The sheik is very interested in rape, but not much troubled by rapists, whom he feels bear an unfair share of the blame. Instead, he believes, it is largely the fault of the woman.

'It is she who takes off her clothes, shortens them, flirts, puts on make-up and powder and takes to the streets, God protect us, dallying,' he said.

I hate that 'dallying', too.

'It's she who shortens, raises and lowers,' said the sheik. 'Then it's a look, then a smile, then a conversation, a greeting, then a conversation, then a date, then a meeting, then a crime, then Long Bay jail.'

The sheik laughed.

'Then you get a judge, who has no mercy, and he gives you 65 years [sic].'

Here he was sniggering at the 55-year sentence originally handed down to his local gang rapist Bilal Skaf.

'They arranged to meet in a public park at 2 or 3am in the morning, and it [the sex] was agreed on,' he said, of an attack in which 14 men raped a young woman 25 times at gunpoint, then washed her down with a hose. 'But when it comes to this disaster, who started it?' the sheik asked, citing the Muslim scholar, al-Rafihi, who believed that if a man kidnapped and raped a woman, the woman should be jailed for life.

'If you take a kilo of meat,' said the sheik, 'and you don't put it in the fridge or in the pot or in the kitchen but you leave it on a plate in the backyard, and then you have a fight with the neighbour because his cats eat the meat, you're crazy. Isn't this true?

'The uncovered meat,' he pronounced, 'is the problem.'

The sheik also ridiculed the idea that a man could be jailed for three and a half years because he raped his wife (or, as the sheik put it, 'Carried out his matrimonial right with his wife without her consent').

These views, of course, do not make him a bastard. It is the role of any religious leader to pontificate nonsensically about sexual morality, to make idiotic social judgements without reference to science or sociology, and to blame everything on women. A mufti — or an archbishop, for that matter — is no more responsible for speaking misogynist gibberish than a cat is guilty for eating meat left out in the backyard. Sadly, however, much of what the sheik said was misinterpreted. Most of the problems of misinterpreting the sheik arise when he speaks Arabic, but the sheik does not like to speak English, so he had a spokesperson, Keysar Trad, to translate everything he said into English, and then say the opposite.

After the sheik's 'uncovered meat' declaration, Keysar said, 'From what I understand, he was talking about the context of encouraging people to abstinence before getting married.'

The sheik and Keysar appeared on the chronically misnamed TV show *A Current Affair* and when the presenter asked whether the sheik thought the uncovered meat was the problem, the sheik replied in Arabic, and Keysar translated. 'He's saying that the man is responsible,' said Keysar, 'that the cat is responsible.'

As to his rapist quip, 'What is meant by that is that anybody who commits the crime of rape deserves 65 years,' said Keysar.

Later, on Egyptian TV, the sheik revealed the truth of life in Australia. 'There are nude beaches in Australia,' he said, 'and if one goes there wearing clothes [one] is fined. And there are streets like that too.'

Australia is home to 'a third sex in between, neither male nor female', said the bearded sheik, wearing a gown.

The sheik blames the media for reporting what he says (instead of what Keysar Trad says he says) and that is why he is a bastard.

Strangely, the sheik is most heavily criticised by people who agree with him, such as **fright-wing columnists**. The month the sheik spoke on Cairo TV, an article appeared in *Quadrant*, the house magazine of the right-wing, 'I'm-a-victim'-whining, middle-class, chardonnay-drinking, latte-sipping, cheese-eating, soon-to-announce-surrender-in-Iraq monkeys, in which Roger Sandall suggested 'it's less than clear that the sheik was entirely wrong'.[1] While that same issue of *Quadrant* was still on the newsstands (because nobody bought it), Sydney fright-winger Miranda Devine wrote, 'In a world saturated with pornography, when women treat themselves like sluts, why would men treat them any differently?'[2]

Thankfully, Miranda and her friends on the *Quadrant* crew are isolated within the Liberal Party, where they have no support.

---

[1] 'The Sexualising of Everyday Life', Roger Sandall, *Quadrant*, Jan–Feb 2007.

[2] 'Losers of the Sexual Revolution', Miranda Devine, *Sydney Morning Herald*, 22/02/07.

silo

noun, **1.** structure essential for preservation of wheat, knowledge etc, prior to dissemination

The dangers posed by silos to the Australian public were first drawn to public attention by the great Australian businessman and satirist, Fred Hilmer. Fred, who was appointed CEO of the publisher John Fairfax in 1998, was concerned that Fairfax journalists had built silos: conical structures found across the Australian wheat belt, and primarily used for the storage of grain. In a similar vein, Erich von Daniken, author of *The Gods were Astronauts*, believed space aliens had erected the Egyptian pyramids.

I have spent several years at Fairfax, and I have never built a silo, nor have I seen anyone else build a silo. During Fred's time at the company's Sydney offices, however, two large structures that looked vaguely like silos — the Imax Theatre and the exhaust tower for the Cross City Tunnel — were built within view of the boardroom. Fred may have believed they were raised by journalists during the lunchbreaks that Fred may have believed journalists took.

In bastardspeak, a silo is held to be a 'management system' that will not work in conjunction with other management systems in the same business. Fred is the former dean of the Australian Graduate School of Management (AGSM), and as such is partly responsible for the topless depth of talent in Australian management today. As a businessperson, he served as deputy chairman of the Foster's Group, and therefore must also take some credit for the high quality and enormous popularity of Foster's Lager in the domestic market.

Once Fred got the job at Fairfax, he quickly felt moved to point out he did not read newspapers much, because he did not have the time. Fred worried that Fairfax did not do enough market research, and the newspapers knew too little about their consumers. He commissioned many expensive studies to find out who were these mysterious people who still had time to read the *Sydney Morning Herald* between their board **meetings** and regular games of **golf**. Under Fred, Fairfax management became intensely interested in questions such as, 'If the *Illawarra Mercury* were a car, what kind of car would it be?'

All this motorphromorphism yielded no useful results whatever. As Fred admitted, during his time as a lone knight tilting his lance at a field of silos, there were no circulation increases 'that could be linked to an editorial initiative'. What Fred discovered was that 'higher circulation was only ever driven by such things as sales and discounting, putting papers in petrol stations and promotional activity'. In other words, the people who bought Fairfax newspapers were of the type who would be more likely to purchase things if they were (a) cheaper; (b) more readily available; or (c) contained free stuff.

Despite his insights, Fred was not a popular figure among the content providers at Fairfax but, after he left the company, he redeemed himself by hiring one of them to co-author *The Fairfax Experience: What the Management Texts Didn't Teach Me*, a hilarious satire based on the premise of a management consultant who does not read newspapers but nonetheless takes over a major Australian media company.

Although he was paid several hundred per cent more than his content providers, this ingeniously painted character did not feel that he, unlike them, was on call 24/7.

In a marvellous passage, the lead character — who is always referred to in the first person, and appears totally unencumbered by self-awareness — complains about discovering that a newspaper's distribution is delayed while he is driving to the links.

'These calls played havoc with my golf game on far too many occasions,' writes Fred. 'The people at the plant knew they could catch me in the car on my way to golf around 7am. After a bad call it would take me four holes to settle down.'

Classic.

sniffer dog

noun, **1.** canine symptom of on-the-nose policing

I was sitting in the upstairs bar of a large and semi-fashionable Sydney pub when I felt a sensation like a midget rubbing his head against my knee. That's strange, I thought. You don't see many midgets around any more. I looked down and noticed a leash. Hmmm. Even if there was a midget population boom, it would probably be illegal to keep them as pets.

It was, in fact, a dog. That's strange, I thought. You don't see many dogs in pubs any more.

At the other end of the leash were five armed police officers, who were weaving a purposeful conga through the crowd of Friday-night drinkers, while their dog stopped at every table to sniff people's knees. After it had sniffed all the straight people's knees, it led its handlers to the rooftop bar, where the other team hangs out.

There is no overestimating the ingenuity of terrorists. Clearly, al-Qaeda fundamentalists in Australia had found the perfect way to spend a teetotal, homophobic night out: drinking beer in a gay bar.

Maybe the cops were on the trail of the little-known 'knee bomber', always one step ahead of Richard Reid, the notorious 'shoe bomber'. But when they emerged from the rooftop bar with no wild-eyed would-be murderer wearing a suicide knee-brace packed with explosives, it seemed the terrorist had escaped to wield his deadly patella another day.

'Nice to see our tax dollars are being well spent,' said my drinking mate.

Of course, the dog was not sniffing for terrorists at all. NSW police, operating under the Police Powers (Drug Detection Dogs) Act 2001, were acting on an anonymous tip-off from a high-level underworld source that students and gay people in the inner city sometimes take party drugs on a Friday night.

The drug most likely to be found on anybody in the pub would be ecstasy or cannabis. Obviously, the police needed to swoop in a five-strong team, in case they were hugged to death by a loved-up pill head, or bored to death by a rambling smoker.

I am not sure this well-planned operation was a useful way to spend that large part of the price of my beer that goes towards paying for stuff I don't want, such as subsidising private schools and destroying Iraq in order to save it. Why aren't the police out with axe-sniffing dogs, searching for axe murderers? Or does nobody commit axe murders any more?

And what exactly are they hoping to accomplish? If the war on drugs is a fight against heroin dealers, they're unlikely to land a heavy blow at 9pm in a pricey hotel. Junkies tend not to go out for a drink on Friday night — particularly to places where a schooner costs $5 — because they're too busy burgling houses. This task is made easier by the fact there are no police patrolling the streets, since they've taken to raiding pubs instead.

Then there's the question of the cops themselves, all of whom looked to be in their early 20s. How many of them had never dropped an E at a party, or unwound with a doobie at the end of a tough shift confiscating other people's doobies? I'm just raising the question.

As for the animals, they are well-trained, clean, obedient and moderately intelligent. They know how to follow orders and quickly learn who is boss. They can be taught to perform many simple tasks that are of great benefit to society.

And the dogs could be more usefully deployed, as well.

Just kidding, readers. Cops are tops. Except for a 'few bad apples'. It's not the fault of the police that they are wasting their time and our money patrolling peaceful pubs in the early evening. The police don't want to squander their nights confiscating drugs from drinkers. They'd rather be selling drugs themselves, like they did in the good old days.

A few months after my sniffer-dog experience, the state ombudsman issued a report that said the sniffer-dog program, which costs more than $1 million a year, had never caught a major criminal. Although more than 10,000 people were searched after being sniffed in the two-year period covered by the report, only a quarter of them were actually carrying drugs and only 19 were prosecuted for supplying; of whom only three were sentenced to periodic detention. Most people who had drugs were carrying 'tiny' amounts of cannabis for personal use.

Fright-wing columnist Miranda Devine responded to the report brilliantly. 'The program works as it should,' she declared. 'Its main usefulness is as a deterrent.'

A couple of months later, the ombudsman revealed that sniffer dogs in NSW, operating under the 2002 Firearms Amendment Act, had probably never found any guns or explosives. They were involved in two successful operations, but each time, it was alleged, the munitions had already been discovered before the dogs arrived.

Once again, the deterrent was working a treat.

sporting song, novelty

noun, **1.** musical curse

Novelty sporting songs are a specialist subcategory of novelty songs. They can, in turn, be divided into two major sub-sub categories: (a) songs ostensibly intended to spur a team — or player — to glorious victory; and (b) songs performed to commemorate a team — or player's — glorious victory.

When you look at the record of category (a) novelty sporting songs, you have to begin to question their effect, if not their actual intent. The last time England won the soccer World Cup was 1966. The tradition of the official song began in 1970.

In 1970, *Back Home*, a clumpingly beautiful gumbie chorus recorded by the England World Cup squad, reached number one in the singles charts. The song reminds me of my dad, and when I hear it in my head (which is the only place I hear it, because it does not get played much on Australian radio) my heart softens and fills with nameless regrets. I suspect it reminds everyone of my generation of their fathers, shivering in heavy coats on the terraces. The evocative *Back Home* boosted the performance of the defending champions to such an extent that England was knocked out of the cup by Germany, the same team it had defeated in the previous finals — and, of course, in two world wars.

Three Lions, the official English soccer European Championship song of 1996, written by comedians David Baddiel and Frank Skinner with music by the Lightning Seeds, reached number one in the UK singles chart, whereas the English European Championship squad went out in the semi-finals — to Germany, of course. Unusually, the song also got to number 16 in the German charts, which is like a promotional song for the US swimming team reaching the Top 20 in Australia.

Three Lions was revamped in 1998, as an 'unofficial anthem' for the English World Cup squad. It got to number one in the charts again, whereas England did not even make the quarter-finals of the tournament. (In a curious geopolitical irony, it was knocked out by Argentina, another country England had previously defeated in war.)

It is possible that a hit song actually sucks the energy out of the team it ostensibly encourages, and the eventual success of the team is in inverse proportion to the sales of the record. There is also a suggestion that military defeats can be reversed by the simple and bloodless expedient of having the Lightning Seeds record a song on behalf of your opponents. The beleaguered 1998 squad was further hampered by its official anthem, the Spice Girls' *(How Does It Feel To Be) On Top Of The World*. Of course, the team never found out.

It should be noted that unofficial soccer songs, such as West Ham United's *I'm Forever Blowing Bubbles*, rarely commit their team to an achievement on the sports field, preferring instead to remind them that their fans will never stop blowing bubbles. This is a great comfort to players, who do not feel under the kind of pressure that might otherwise prove psychologically damaging.

Australia has *Up There Cazaly*, a category (b) tune celebrating the achievements of AFL great Roy Cazaly. While not quite in the premier league of novelty sporting songs, *Cazaly* is quite a good second-grade district amateur, especially considering that it was written and performed by singer-songwriter Mike Brady, who did not like AFL and had never watched a game. His ignorance of the traditions of the sport might explain his heartless exhortation to a man who had been dead for 16 years to get 'in there and fight'. At least Paul Kelly's unusual ballad *Bradman* did not seek to encourage the Don to step back to the crease and hit an England player with his bat.

In March 1994, veteran Aussie pop singer Doug Parkinson released a tribute to cricket captain Allan Border, entitled *Where Would We Be Without AB?* In April 1994, Allan Border answered his question by retiring from international cricket.

stranger, conversation-starting

noun, **1.** enemy you just haven't met yet

I met a bloke once on a plane who got me so drunk that I can't remember his name. I was allocated a seat facing the curtain that separates the corporate criminals in business class from the poor-but-honest, salt-of-the-earth types in economy. The guy next to me had forearms like thighs, and said he worked in a mining camp. When the plane took off, he dived into business class to use their diamond-encrusted toilets. I offered him a beer, and he feigned horror when I handed the hostie my money. He never paid for his beer on planes, he said. They don't keep records of how many drinks are given away in business class and how many are sold in economy. The staff just pocket the takings, to save the trouble of doing the books — and if they like you, they'll give you drinks for free.

Yeah, right.

When he called for a round, the hosties gave it to him for free, on the unlikely pretence that we had asked for two cans of Foster's but they were only able to produce one Foster's and one Toohey's New. My next round was free, too, presumably on grounds of precedence. After that, I gave up even trying to pay, and simply concentrated on getting my no-money's worth.

My new buddy was a passable raconteur, and he told me several stories I've since forgotten. It was a throwback to the great days of smoking **cigarettes** on planes, when all the interesting people were crowded into the back rows. Not everyone who drank was a smoker, but everyone who smoked was a drinker. Beers were complimentary, and briefly we were all as rich as **Alexander Downer**. You could stand a round for your whole row and still arrive home with change from nothing.

When I mentioned this to the mine engineer, he announced he was gasping for a smoke, jogged down to the economy-class bathroom, disabled the smoke alarm, and had half a cigarette. I was asthmatic with admiration.

But I'm old enough to know you don't meet your new best friend on a plane. True friendships are forged in struggles against bosses, teachers, parents, and ginger-haired kids in the playground. The guy you chat with over a beer might be okay for the first six drinks, but by the lucky seventh, it always turns out he doesn't like gays, blacks, Jews, Asians, Aborigines or Arabs — and whoever it is he has a problem with, he can't shut up about them.

I'm bored with arguing with bigots. I usually get up and walk out of the door. I try not to do this on aeroplanes, however.

My seat-mate had issues with women, and once he started on about them, he wouldn't talk about anything else, despite my quiet attempts to turn the conversation into a discussion of Australia's roundest roundabouts or something.

By the time we landed, we were barely speaking. It was all a little sad, in a desultory, predictable way. But hey, thanks for the free drinks.

stranger, fight-starting

noun, **1.** extremist version of the above. **2.** fundamentalist stranger

I have often been offered fights by passers-by. It's something about my face. My nose is crooked and my chin is lopsided, perhaps giving the impression that a decent right cross would knock everything back into place.

I was once sitting at the bar of the Quarrymen's Arms in Pyrmont, when a man came up and said, 'I think your wife's got beautiful eyes.'

'Thank you,' I said.

'No, mate,' he said. '*I think your wife's got beautiful eyes.*'

'So do I,' I said, although I would've been hard pressed to say what colour they were.

'Let's have a fight,' said the wife-complimenting stranger.

No.

'Oh come on,' he said, 'we can go outside, punch each other for a bit, then put our arms around each other and be mates.'

It was an enticing prospect, but I had to decline. He crossed to the saloon bar, and made the same offer to two blokes in blue overalls.

I was walking out of the toilets in the old Rex Hotel in Kings Cross, when a guy told me to button up my fly, then asked, 'Do you and your mate want to fight me and my mate?'

No.

'But we're from *New Zealand*,' he said, as if they had come all the way to Sydney just to beat us up, and now I had ruined their holiday.

At a pub in Rushcutters Bay, somebody dispensed with the preliminaries and just threw a beer can at me.

I used to live in Redfern, which is still one of the best places in Sydney to get into a misunderstanding. One evening my then-girlfriend persuaded me to go to a fancy-dress party as Zorro. I strode proudly through the Redfern night in my black blouson, black breeches, black boots and black hat, with my trusty plastic sword in its black plastic sheath, when I realised I didn't have a match for my **cigarette**.

I asked a passing smoker if I could have a light.

'No,' he said.

'Why not?' I stammered, astounded.

He looked at my outfit with magnificent disdain.

'Because you're a fucking poofter,' he said.

sushi

***noun*, 1.** raw fish

It's raw fish. *Raw fish*, don't you get it? Oh, never mind.

taxi driver, Melbourne

noun, **1.** same as any other taxi driver, but possessed of an incomprehensible, unnecessary and improperly utilised system of rooftop lights that confounds locals and visitors alike, and allows the driver to cruise past would-be passengers in the rain with an unapologetic half-smile and no visually coherent explanation

taxi driver, Sydney

noun, **1.** same as any other taxi driver, but with no idea where he is going

Learn a bit of local geography before you apply for a cab licence, mate. And turn off the fucking radio, eh?

taxi driver, Western Australian

noun, **1.** quasi-mythical beast, believed to have existed in large areas of WA in the years before the resources boom

Fossils thought to belong to the Western Australian taxi driver have been found throughout the state, and bear a striking resemblance to unskilled workers in the Kimberley and Pilbara regions in the modern era. Parts of WA continue to sustain small, cargo-cult-style groups of pedestrians, who persist in the belief that the taxi drivers will return one day. They gather in hopeful queues at around midnight in cities and towns, and only disperse when they have all been beaten up, robbed or raped.

tea tree oil

noun, **1.** snake oil

team building

noun, **1.** way of forcing people who do not necessarily like each other to spend a weekend together for no financial reward, doing something that none of them wants to do. **2.** nothing, a waste of time

team player

noun, **1.** something bastards claim to be in job interviews. **2.** the kind of person **human resources** is looking for to fill a 'vacancy'. **3.** a member of sports teams with no particular talent. **4.** somebody incapable of doing his job on his own, and therefore forced to rely on subordinates to do it for him

teetotaller

noun, **1.** terrorist, dictator

Most terrorists are **beard**ed teetotallers. I, too, would probably want to blow myself up, if I walked around all day with half a sheep hanging from my chin and I could not relax in the evening with a cold beer and 12 bottles of wine. It can be no coincidence that both Adolf Hitler and Osama bin Laden were teetotallers.

Of course, not all teetotallers — perhaps even not most of them — are mass murderers, but you certainly have more time to plan the destruction of civilisation on the planet if you are sober.

There is no evidence that the Salvation Army is a terrorist organisation as such, but it celebrates three of the most savage blights on contemporary society: religion, militarism and temperance. These days, the Salvationists move unmolested through city pubs, selling their aggressively named publication *War Cry* and generally looking grim, drawn and inexplicably dehydrated, like prison warders who have been left out in the sun.

There was a time, however, when the drinking population actually got it together for long enough to drive them from the streets.

The Skeleton Army was formed in the late 19th century with the selfless assistance of publicans, butchers and brewers. It stood for the inviolable 'three Bs' — beer, beef and baccy — published its own obscene publications, and marched against the

Salvationists with the cheerful violence that is the hallmark of most large public gatherings in England.

In the US, the Industrial Workers of the World, nicknamed the Wobblies, hoped to organise the entire working class into one single trade union, by means of wobbling. (The IWW is still valiantly quivering towards its noble goal, with about 2000 members internationally, and is expected to reach critical mass some time after a comet hits the earth and wipes out humanity.) The bosses used to hire the Salvation Army band to drown out the speakers at Wobbly meetings, so the Wobblies wrote their own lyrics to the Salvos' songs, such as *Hallelujah I'm A Bum*.

In those days, the menace of teetotallers was widely recognised among the most progressive elements of society. Today, they move among us like fish in mineral water, planning their next atrocity over glasses of iced tea.

trivia 'nites'

noun, **1.** social outings for slime

Trivia has been the stuff of pub conversation since the beginning of time (which happened around 1963, when The Beatles released *She Loves You* and, uncoincidentally, I was born), but it became institutionalised when the now-forgotten 'trivia machines' appeared in hotel bars in the UK in the 1980s. These machines were an offshoot of the Trivial Pursuit craze, and offered multiple-choice answers to fairly easy questions. One question was 'What is the biggest dog in the world?' Sample answers included 'the Indian mega dog'. They were set at just the right level for the average pub intellectual (ie low) and were meant to entertain and inform the existing patrons, rather than drag in non-drinkers off the street. You used to be able to win money on the trivia machines, so enterprising young men would stand patiently watching every player, every day, memorising every answer, until they could beat the machine every time. Pub trivia machines disappeared just before mobile phones and the internet would have killed them anyway, but not before a pub-trivia culture was established in many hotels.

History repeats itself irritatingly, like **Santo Santoro**'s name. When live trivia nights first came to city pubs across the globe, they were intended as entertainment for the punters, a chance to win a bit of cash or a crate of beer. Most pubs did not limit team members' numbers, so savvy punters quickly realised the easy way to win was to get together a really big team. As the teams grew bigger, the questions grew harder, but then something strange happened: teams reached a critical mass. At a certain point, it did not help to take on any more players. Even if the entire pub turned on the quizmaster, it would be incapable of agreeing on the correct answer to a simple question.

Then, as if by evolutionary imperative, a new breed of human slime spewed out of the gutters, having spent decades living in sewers with their sweated-over dictionaries, piss-stained encyclopaedias, shit-smeared almanacs and snot-soaked records books. They had festered in the damp and the dark, eating rats and drinking their own urine, never cutting their hair or washing

217

their flared trousers, devoting every squalid moment of their fetid existence to memorising cricket scores, or learning by heart the 25 longest rivers in the world. They reproduced asexually and spawned creatures without genitals, without hairstyles, without fashion sense and without friends. But they knew every fact about everything. Just one of these trivia insects could defeat a team of ten ordinary nerds, and go back home to their stormwater drain with a $50 note and six pack of VB in their plastic shopping bag.

I began to avoid pubs on trivia 'nite'. (Why don't they ever ask the question, What is the correct spelling of 'night'? Eh? Eh?) Sometimes, however, the pub just springs it on you. At 8pm, an out-of-work actor who performs as a singing telegram six nights a week hands you a photocopied sheet of paper with blurry pictures of Ronald Reagan, Neil Armstrong, Donna Summer and the bloke who invented the Hill's Hoist, and asks if you want to 'play'. In the time before the trivia insects, the questions would have been 'Who was this American president and why did he want to blow up the world?' etc. These days, you'd be lucky to get, 'Ronald Reagan (pictured) was the 40th president of the United States. Name the other 39.'

There is some serious trivia that needs to be discussed in pubs. I often find myself groping for an answer to a query such as, 'Who was that bloke, you know, the one that used to go around with that other bloke, who went out with that girl who wore that jacket? She didn't work in Woolworth's, but it was somewhere like that…?' when my answer is drowned out by a bonus-round question about the second-largest mountain in Chile.

Last year, with all this in mind, I still asked my mate Patrick if he wanted to come to the rock trivia quiz at the Sandringham Hotel in Newtown, Sydney. Rock or 'pop' trivia games were a new phenomenon; therefore, judging by the history of trivia, the questions should have been easy. The theme of the quiz was 'the vinyl years'. I'd never been before, but I knew we would win, because I am the Rock Brain of Australia, the real person on whom the fictitious character of Glenn A. Baker is based.

And we did win. We won four Rick Astley 12-inch singles (who would have guessed he'd made *four*?) as a prize for coming last. In addition, we were awarded an LP called *'87 Hots Up*, featuring the biggest hits of 1987, as a prize for coming last in the bonus round. That was our final humiliation, like taking a kick to the head when we'd already been shot, stabbed, strangled and made to listen to four Rick Astley 12-inch singles.

Patrick also managed to win a Simple Minds LP, obscurely bestowed for making up a joke about The Beatles. It didn't really matter how many records we were given, though, since neither of us owns a record player.

The quiz defeated us in part because it was a special '80s night. The '80s is colloquially known as 'the decade Mark Dapin forgot', since I spent 1984–1988 in a sustained drunken despair. Patrick and I averaged three out of ten correct answers, falling to a spectacular one out of ten in the bonus round. We knew nothing.

Almost a week later, Patrick rang and told me he had figured out why we had failed: we had *picked the wrong name for our team*. We had gone in as 'Wham!', with Patrick playing a blond George Michael to my dark-haired Andrew Ridgeley.

He insisted we go back and try again. We took Jack Marx. We called ourselves 'I, Spartacus', after Jack's ill-known Newcastle rock band. We protested answers. We cheated. And we still finished second-from-last. I came home with a live album by Peggy Lee and George Shearing. I'd rather have **gout**.

In the end, the pub is not for people who enjoy organised activities. It is a sanctuary from **team players** and **people persons**. Drinkers go to pubs to kill brain cells, not to exercise them. Trivia insects do not drink beer, because it clouds their minds, and their presence encourages humans to abstain, too, in the mistaken belief that it will give them a chance against this most horrible mutation of the social drinker.

Pub trivia 'nites' are a boil on the buttock of pub culture. They are, however, a useful excuse to go out for a drink in the early part of the week and not come back until the 'last round' is over.

unAustralian

noun, **1.** not a real Australian, such as a foreigner, a trade unionist, an Aboriginal person etc. **2.** an Australian

Take a long, sideways look at the people around you. They may be wearing Australian clothes, talking in Australian accents, discussing uniquely Australian topics (such as the inexplicable and unprecedented nature of drought) but they might not be Australian at all. They could be part of that growing national minority, the UnAustralians.

'UnAustralian' is an old term given new life during the 1990s boom in unhelpful communication, which also brought us the phrase 'political correctness' and sudden rise of **air punctuation**.

'UnAustralian' comes to the fore in times of social upheaval. It ridiculed radicals when the diggers came back from the trenches to face the new threat of communism at home; when strikers fought for workers' rights during the 1920s; and when home-grown right-wing militia organised against 'cosmopolitan' socialists in the lead-up to World War II.

Prime Minister Stanley Bruce announced his intention to rid the country of 'unAustralian' troublemakers in 1925. Tommy White, a minister of the Lyons government of the 1930s, wanted to keep out 'unAustralian' groups such as 'the non-British', and also 'the disloyal, the subversive and seditious [communists], and the criminal'.

After a brief popularity in the paranoid, patriotic Menzies era, 'unAustralian' appears to have lain dormant during the '60s and '70s, possibly revived by then-Opposition leader John Howard when he decried as 'unAustralian' proposals for an Australia Card in the mid-'80s.

Even so, for a time John seemed uncomfortable with the term. During the Mabo case, when it looked as if Australia's first people were setting themselves up as the arbiters of what was and was not Australian, John said, 'This is a classic McCarthyist technique. One wonders how long it will be before the establishment of an unAustralian activities committee is proposed.'

These days, John trusts no one, and often seems on the verge of establishing such a committee himself, just as he is introducing the Australia Card by another name.

UnAustralians have infiltrated our society at every level, and the prime minister seems to have become especially adept at spotting them. In 1996, he labelled trade unionists who attacked Parliament House 'unAustralian'. In 1997, he detected UnAustralians among the detractors of cricket captain Mark Taylor. The same year, he called street campaigns against Pauline Hanson 'unAustralian'. Most famously, in 2000, he realised the S11 anti-globalisation protesters were unAustralian.

West Australian premier Richard Court also commented on the unAustralian nature of the S11 demonstrators. Victorian premier Steve Bracks, supposedly from the other side of politics, noticed they were unAustralian, too.

The demonstrators themselves seemed bewildered by their re-branding. Scott Alderson, producer of the compilation rock CD *UnAustralian*, told me, 'I remember being at the anti-globalisation protests outside the World Economic Forum in Melbourne, and every politician used the word "unAustralian" to describe the people outside ... The majority of people inside were representatives of international companies, and the people outside were Australians concerned about local issues and national sovereignty.'

Even stranger was the accusation by multinational credit card company Visa International that the Reserve Bank of Australia was 'unAustralian'.

Sharp-eyed politicians throughout the nation joined in the hunt for unAustralians, but it was not until clear-thinking Northern Territory government minister Mark Read realised that Aborigines themselves were unAustralian (when they tried to stop tourists from climbing Uluru during a period of mourning) that the true scope of the infiltration problem became clear.

Meanwhile, Greens senator Bob Brown called the Northern Territory government's mandatory sentencing laws 'unAustralian' when a 29-year-old Aboriginal man received a 12-month jail sentence for stealing a towel from a clothesline to use as a blanket.

The word unAustralian is like a boomerang. When you throw it, it comes back to you. Dozens of commentators have suggested John Howard himself is unAustralian. Simon Crean said it was unAustralian that the government was bugging phone calls to the *Tampa*. Janet Holmes à Court said it was unAustralian that an Australian could not be the Australian head of state.

Meanwhile, Paul Keating had been attacked as unAustralian by Kerry Jones, head of Australians for Constitutional Monarchy, when he refused to become a Companion of the Order of Australia because it was an imperial honour.

The cycle was not broken until Alan Fels accused the big oil companies of being unAustralian when they raised the price of petrol by eight cents a litre on Anzac Day. In response, Malcolm Irving of Caltex Australia magnificently called his critics 'billygoats'.

The lesson is clear. UnAustralians lurk in every corner of society, and Australians who call other Australians 'unAustralian' are just as likely to be UnAustralian themselves. UnAustralians must be sent back to UnAustralia, whence they came. They are not welcome here, because they do not subscribe to Australian values, such as making people welcome here.

In the times ahead, it will be every citizen's duty to root out and expose UnAustralians, wherever they may be. And when we've got them all sorted out, we can start on the billygoats.

unproductive profession

noun, 1. job, the characteristics of which are not immediately apparent from the title, in which the performance of the job holder cannot be gauged by any recognised means

If somebody says he is a coal miner, he mines coal. If somebody says she is a teacher, she teaches. If somebody says they are a chief knowledge officer, a chief visionary officer or a chief learning officer, they don't do anything.

They are too busy being bastards.

vanstone

verb, 1. to put something back where it does not belong. Eg 'She vanstoned Dan Brown's *Da Vinci Code* to the literary-fiction section of the bookshop'

The extraordinary Amanda Vanstone, the former minister for immigration and multicultural affairs, looks like a wedding cake dropped on a chicken factory. Under her stewardship, the immigration department developed a range of innovative policies including one that allowed for the arbitrary return of naturalised Australian citizens to their country of origin, and another that saw overseas-born mentally ill residents locked up in detention centres.

While she was immigration minister, Amanda continued her taxpayer-funded education as if she were still at private school. She spent at least $30,000 of taxpayers' money on lessons in Mandarin Chinese, apparently believing Mandarin to be the national language of Italy. When she finally 'left' her ministerial position, Amanda was appointed Australia's ambassador to Italy, in preparation for which she began taking taxpayer-funded Italian lessons.

Although 800,000 Australians claim Italian descent, no Italian-speaking Australian could be found to fill the position, because she had vanstoned them all to detention centres for the duration of the selection process.

War on Terror

***noun*, 1.** conflict unlikely to be won due to the difficulty of subduing an evolutionarily conditioned response

A war with an emotion is likely to end in tears. Terror itself made the first move in the War on Terror, when a bunch of hijackers, mostly nationals of **Saudi Arabia**, flew US passenger jets into the Twin Towers and the Pentagon on September 11. The US struck back by invading Afghanistan, which is quite near Saudi Arabia, as the crow flies.

In Afghanistan, the psychotic jihadist regime of the Taliban, which insisted all men should wear **beards**, had diplomatic recognition only from the governments of **Saudi Arabia**, the

UAE and Pakistan, all western allies in the War on Terror. Even though the Taliban were Sunni Muslims, they were not recognised by Sunni Muslim death beast Saddam Hussein, and they were mortal enemies of the Axis of Evil Shi'a regime in Iran.

The US Army assembled in Saudi Arabia and the most powerful military in the world quickly succeeded in forcing the mastermind of Terror, Osama bin Laden, to move house. The US also killed heaps of Afghans, who hailed them as liberators from the Taliban, a government educated in Islamic schools in Pakistan funded by Saudi Arabia, which ruled the country with no support from its people.

We were not always at war with terror. When bearded Mujahideen resistance medievalists — including Osama bin Laden — were fighting to drive the Soviets out of Afghanistan in the 1980s, we thought terror was a good mate to have around in a tight situation, although we wouldn't necessarily have invited him back for a barbie. The West secretly armed and trained the Mujahideen, who had launched an Islamist uprising against the murderous but secular Afghan government of the PDPA (People's Democratic Party of Afghanistan), which had no support from the Afghan people, which is why it is important to bring democracy to the Middle East.

It was not always important to bring democracy to the Middle East. The only democratically elected government of Iran, led by Mohammed Mossadegh, was overthrown by the CIA in 1953, when it nationalised the oil company that was to become BP. Mohammed was replaced by a feudal monarch, the Shah, who returned part of BP, but was later overthrown by a feudal cleric, the Ayatollah, who took it back again.

Although today it is much more important to bring democracy to the Middle East than it used to be, it is equally important that the Arabs do not use democracy to elect people who have no support among the Arab people, such as Hamas in Palestine. In cases like this, it is best to try to starve the Arabs into holding another election. This can continue indefinitely, until such time as they finally vote for someone who has support among them, such as George Bush, who is a hero to the Iraqi people after liberating them from Saddam Hussein.

After invading Afghanistan, the US invaded Iraq. Under Saddam Hussein, who ruled the country with no support from its people, Iraq was a state sponsor of terror. His terror was against Israel, not the US, and took the form of providing pensions for the families of Palestinian suicide bombers. Suicide bombers find it notoriously difficult to get life insurance, so Saddam's magnanimous provisions made him popular in the Arab world, where he had no support.

Among the many Iraqis who did not support Saddam were the 600,000–700,000 people estimated[1] by US intelligence to belong to the Ba'ath Party; the 385,000 soldiers in the Iraqi Army; and the 335,000 members combined of the police and security forces, and their families. This is why it was possible to fight a war against them for their own benefit, although it was unfortunately necessary to take away their jobs at the end of it.

Saddam was one of the most evil dictators in world history, but the refugees who fled his wicked regime were, if anything, even worse. They were just a bunch of queue-jumping, dole-bludging

[1] Cited in Thomas E. Rick's *Fiasco: The American Military Adventure in Iraq*.

spies, who would drown their own children if they thought that would get them a corporation house in Orange and a job driving cabs. If they had been genuine refugees, they would have applied for asylum while they were still in Iraq, and formed an orderly queue while Saddam put them through the giant people-mincing machine that it turned out he did not really have.

The Australian government discouraged people from leaving Iraq, then attacked those who stayed there. It did this because it was against Terror.

As for al-Qaeda, every time they appear on the news, we see the same 'training video' of men in pyjamas swinging on a climbing frame. In the next scene, they probably jump on a roundabout, or play in the sandpit. What kind of operation are they training for? It looks like an obstacle race, or a primary-school sports day for insomniacs. There is not an aeroplane in sight. It is all very well securing airports, but what is being done to protect our children's playgrounds from terrorism?

More to the point, why did we declare a War on Terror instead of a War on al-Qaeda, as **beard**ed a bunch of **teetotal** bastards as you will find anywhere in the world?

We might even have won.

water-cooler moment

noun, **1.** moment in which somebody goes to the water-cooler to get a glass of cool water

Not so long ago, people who marketed to men often said they wanted their product talked about in the pub. They had in mind a mutant, bastard's version of a pub, where well-dressed, well-spoken young men sat around a table saying things like, 'I'm so much more comfortable with my anus since I started using Action Sports Hemorrhoid Cream for Men.'

These days, bastards' attention has shifted to the water-cooler, which they imagine to be a sort of modern-day milk bar, where clean-living, fresh-faced media consumers gather to discuss the previous night's television.

In fact, aside from complaining about work, bosses, HR etc, the following exchanges are most likely to occur at the water-cooler.

Woman to woman: 'What *is* she wearing?'

Man to woman: 'Can I see you after work?'

Lunatic to water-cooler: 'I'm so much more comfortable with my anus since I started using Action Sports Hemorrhoid Cream for Men.'

Man to man: nothing.

xylophone

***noun,* 1.** tokenistic musical instrument used to fill the space reserved for words beginning with 'x' in dictionaries, mock dictionaries and books like this one. **2.** transparent attempt by the sinister letter 'x' to shore up its status in the world of lexicography

One 26th of a child's alphabet-learning time is devoted to memorising the word 'xylophone', which (a) is of no use to anybody; and (b) calls into question the entire basis of a 26-letter alphabet. If 'x' — as in xylophone — is pronounced the same way as 'z', why bother with both letters? In fact, why bother with anything? We might as well all just go home and die. It's not as if 'z' needs any help bearing its load. It's already the most underused letter in the English language.

Most of the words used to teach a child the alphabet could reasonably be expected to play a part in its adult life. That 'A is for apple' is a useful thing to know, for example, particularly if you are buying an iPod. As the alphabet progresses, the examples become ever more peripheral to actual childhood experience, and encourage unrealistic expectations of the adult world. A kid learning the alphabet would be entitled to expect to see at least as many xylophones and zebras in the world as apples. In fact, there is no country on earth where this is the case.

Appendix A: The 13 Kinds of Beard

Surprisingly, in these decimalised days, there are an unlucky 13 types of beard.

Aboriginal beard

Australia's first beard is still its most impressive. The awesome beards of Aboriginal activist Pat Dodson and the late storyteller Burnum Burnum hang proud in defiance of two centuries of European barber shops. These national treasures lend gravity to the righteous pronouncements of their owners, in much the same way as they lend credence to the theory of gravity by growing downwards instead of upwards. Aboriginal elders' beards are the stalactites of the bearded world: untold centuries in the making, unparalleled in nature and completely in harmony with their environment.

journalistic beard

Men-in-black Phillip Adams and Paddy McGuinness are rarely seen together. This was long thought to be due to personal and political antipathy between the teetotal, left-wing commentator and the social drinking right-winger. In fact, it is because they share the same beard. There is only one neatly trimmed, white beard available to newspaper columnists. Although Paddy, as a former editor-in-chief of the *Australian Financial Review*, has priority, he is obliged to hand it over to Phillip if the latter can demonstrate proven need. Paddy refuses to groom the beard during his tenure, leaving it to Phillip to regularly trim the edges. The two men also share a shirt and trousers.

scientists' beard

A scientist's beard is rugged and unkempt, signalling his contempt for irrational mores such as shaving, his legendary absent-mindedness and his penchant for experimentation. A scientist cannot help but wonder what difference it would make if the front of his head looked the same as the back. To appear even cleverer than they are, bearded scientists put their spectacles on backwards and wander around the laboratory making unlikely observations about objects that are ostensibly behind them. The two main subsets of scientists — mad professors and evil geniuses — invariably wear beards, usually pointy ones.

fugitives' beard

The most blatant use of the beard for underhand purposes is that practised by the prison escapee. Labouring under the misapprehension that a man who looks as if he is halfway through eating a cat will attract no attention, bearded escapees are always recaptured — look at Brad Pitt in the movie *The Devil's Own*. In an amazing application of modern technology, the police force is now able to use high-tech equipment to create computer-generated images of what a fugitive might look like if he were to grow facial hair. This is not the same, of course, as getting an old photograph and scribbling a beard on it.

goatee

Rock stars have them — George Michael and the late Kurt Cobain; movie types have them — Johnny Depp and Spike Lee; people who serve in cafes have them; even Satan wears one. Traditionally an artist's beard, the goatee is usually well-kept to distinguish it from a scientist's unruly shrubbery. It loiters around the jaw like a tramp outside a bottle shop. Without the suspension of sideburns, the goatee — like the tramp — looks as if it might drop off at any time.

legal beard

Just as owners begin to look like their pets and scientists like the result of their experiments, criminal lawyers often end up resembling their clients. When asked which of his distinguished customers are most likely to be bearded, Andrew Tolley of Melbourne's pre-eminent gentlemen's hairdresser Geo. F. Trumper told me: 'Barristers and QCs. If you walk around the chambers you'll see heaps of them with beards, mainly the ones over 50. [They favour] fairly full ones.' The legal beard demonstrates an understanding of the mechanics of crime: should a bearded barrister need to go on the run, all he has to do is shave to render himself unrecognisable.

clerical beard

God himself has a beard, but then God rarely has to go for a job interview or impress women at parties. Jesus, the son of God, inherited the family beard, as did subsequent holy men and God's earlier confidants such as Moses, memorably mimicked by Charlton Heston in *The Ten Commandments*.

Rabbis and imams are also unlikely to be caught with Gillettes in the shopping trolley. Interestingly, the founders of new religions tend to favour chin lichen, from Shoko Asahara of the Japanese sect Aum Shinrikyo to David Koresh of the ill-fated Branch Davidians.

Lincoln beard

Abraham Lincoln was the first US president to be assassinated and the only one to have a beard named after him. Born in a log cabin, Lincoln apparently remained faithful to his log-cabin barber all his life. The Lincoln beard is chiefly notable for its absence of moustache — a small step in the right direction. The Lincoln beard never became a generic political beard. The man who freed the slaves seemed a hard act to follow — until the advent of the Whitlam government, when Moss Cass, one-time environment minister, felt he was man enough to ape Big Abe.

hairdressers' beard

Sydney barber Emmanuel Rantzos, who has occasionally cut my hair, has worn an immaculate hybrid goatee for 45 years. 'I don't remember myself without it,' he says. What beard best suits a professional? 'It's up to the individual face,' says Emmanuel.

Clean-shaven Andrew Tolley of Geo. F. Trumper offers these rules: 'Keeping clean is the main thing, and making sure the hair does not irritate the skin underneath. At least get it properly trimmed. You should shave underneath your collar to add some sort of definition ... Prince Michael of Kent's beard is probably the most refined in the world today — slightly pointed at the bottom, fairly close but thickly grown.'

lower-lip bit

Neither bearded not beardless, the confused youths who wear a single, vertical strip of hair beneath their lower lip will probably end up in mental hospitals or, at the very least, in loveless marriages. Poor old Bob Geldof. These people are so confounded by the pace and complexity of modern life, they cannot make even the most simple decision: to shave or not to shave. They are ambidextrous floating voters, dual nationals, back-seat drivers, damp squibs and ditherers, incapable of committing themselves to a relationship or a single course of action. Their perversion is so bizarre that, like the desire to have sex with insects, it does not even have a name.

alien beard

As a rule, aliens do not wear beards. When you have a brain shaped like a rugby ball, transparent skin, eyes on stalks and claws for hands, it would be illogical to compound your image problem by hanging a shag-pile carpet from your chin. The

Klingons in *Star Trek* are the exception to the universal rule. Once an expansionist evil empire, the Klingon race has been partially rehabilitated but will never be trusted entirely until it reveals its upper lip and jawline. Notably, the Klingons were given beards to make them look grotesque.

Quaker beard

Long a favourite among gentle, non-conformist, God-fearing folk such as the Amish and the Quakers, this beard looks like a halo worn as a bonnet. It bestows a holy glow on its ascetic acolytes. The writer Thomas Keneally — who is about as far from a bastard as you can possibly get — is Australia's most prominent wearer of the Quaker beard. But it was also the foliage of choice of the incomparably evil villain in the brilliant Dutch-language version of the movie *The Vanishing*.

terrorists' beard

What do the following have in common? Unshaven Irish republican gunmen of the 1970s; Osama bin Laden; Satwant and Beant Singh, who assassinated Mrs Gandhi; and Yigal Amir, who shot Yitzhak Rabin. That's right. Catholic, Muslim, Sikh or Jew, every one of them wore a beard as a proud symbol of his murderous ambitions. In Afghanistan — when it was a terrorist state — the Taliban insisted all men should wear long beards.

(In Albania, by contrast, under the enlightened regime of Enver Hoxha, men with beards were made to shave them off before they entered the country. And in Turkmenistan, under the brilliant Turkmenbashi, young men were banned from growing them.)

All terrorists wear beards to disguise themselves. If you see a picture of a terrorist without a beard he either (a) is innocent; or (b) has shaved off his beard to disguise himself.

Appendix B: A List of Imaginary Countries that Should Exist in Preference to Belarus

Tired of the same old boring overseas getaways? Why not spend next year's holiday in a country that doesn't exist?

Interested in Islam and architecture, but don't fancy getting stoned to death every time you go out for a drink? Try **Gaudi Arabia**, a Mecca for tourists and pilgrims alike. The holiest Muslim shrines line the same streets as delirious churches and sensuous apartments created by Catalunya's visionary architect, Antoni Gaudi. And there's no hajji-bargy about alcohol here. The whole nation is subject to Spain's liberal licensing laws. Dance until dawn in the tapas bars of Riyadh, the city that never sleeps. Surely this is one nation that deserves its nickname — 'Rowdy Arabia', the nightlife capital of the Middle East.

In neighbouring **Afghanistanada**, the harsh strictures of sharia law have been replaced by an easygoing Canadian attitude to life. Bearded locals play ice hockey in the desert, in the shadow of large and un-blown-up statues of the Buddha. There's no Osama bin Laden lurking here, plotting to ruin everyone's holiday by hijacking their planes and flying them into tall buildings. The reassuring presence of the Royal Canadian Mounted Mujahideen (or 'Mudgees') sees to that.

Frustrated with France? There's always **Deli France**. It's just like Paris, except there's adequate provision of toilets, the staff don't pretend not to understand English, and the croissants taste sort of rubbery. And it doesn't close for four hours in the middle of the day, just when you fancy a bit of cake for afternoon tea.

Perhaps you love windmills, dykes and tulips, but also enjoy classic r'n'b? Visit **Holland–Dozier–Holland**, a confederation of three independent states, two of which were mistakenly given the same name by lazy, drunken geographers. Although Holland is the largest of the trio, culturally eclipsing both Dozier and Holland, each country has its own unique Motown heritage. In Dozier, for instance, R. Dean Taylor, the first white artist to sign to the Detroit label, is worshipped as a god.

In Asia, there's **Burmany** (nobody calls it by its new name, Myanmunich), where the mysterious temples of an ancient civilisation are serviced by the finest roads in Europe. Take the autobahn to Mandalay, and relive Kipling's dramatic poem in Teutonic comfort.

There's no need to agonise over Aung Sang Su Kyi: she's the president of the Burmese Bundestag. The only 'house arrest' she worries about is how to give an 'arresting' performance in the lower house.

Looking for something more familiar? There's always **Transylvania Waters**, Aussie suburbia in the black heart of Europe. Join Noelene for a midi of blood at the local RSL, as colourful peasants on horses and carts perform burn-outs and donuts in the car park. Drop in on 'The Castle Dracula', which the knockabout Dracula family saved from demolition and redevelopment as an airport runway. Be sure to carry a garlic-based repellent.

Closer to home, there's the Palestine of the Pacific, **Jew Caledonia**, where Jews and Kanaks live together in perfect harmony, like keys on a piano. They even celebrate 'Kananka' together when the rest of the world thinks it is Christmas. Don't 'passover' this unique cultural experience — it's only a three-hour flight from Sydney. Warning: for cultural reasons, this nation is never referred to by its initials, 'JC'.

Why not combine a week in Jew Caledonia with a weekend in **Vanuatunisia**, where Muslims and Melanesians also live together in perfect harmony, also like keys on a piano? Surely, these two small countries are an example to the world, the very model of the multiracial paradise that Paul McCartney envisaged when he went to live on his own on a private island in the North Sea.

Nearby **Nauruganda** is often cited as the 'next big destination' for refugees. So what if we mined all its phosphate and filled the holes with asylum seekers? It still boasts vast swathes of unspoiled jungle, populated by majestic families of mountain gorillas. Watch bewildered Iraqis stare at the wildlife from behind barbed wire. They think they're in Queensland. They think the chimpanzees are kangaroos. They think we're going to let them out.

They were trying to reach **Lostralia**, a wide, brown land with only one previous, careful owner, where everyone gets a fair go — even if they arrive by boat. It is an open, tolerant country with a strong egalitarian spirit. Of course, it does not really exist.

Appendix C: How to be a Celebrity

For those keen to escape the obscurity of their day-to-day existence, and taste the succulent fruits of faux fame, there are ten (of course) simple steps to the F-list.

Stand next to somebody famous

In March 2001, celebrity agent Max Markson was asked to help Tasmanian model Prue Jackson get publicity in Sydney. He invited her to a charity tribute to Col Joye, took her to the VIP area and posed her next to **Bob Carr**, Col Joye, Steve Liebmann, Brian Henderson and any other man who was standing still. The next morning, the gossip-column picture desks buckled under the weight of photos of this unknown pneumatic blonde with a succession of bewildered middle-aged blokes in suits.

A tabloid social page ran several of the pictures. Unfortunately for Prue, the page was headlined 'Who's That Girl?' and her face was obscured with a question mark each time it appeared.

Part-time model, columnist, radio announcer and author and full-time famous person Bessie Bardot told me, 'Probably the best example of me standing next to someone was when I was photographed with Richard Branson at the launch of the new Virgin Mobile. He was standing at the door, I was walking in, wearing a black busty top, and I shook his hand, and that picture was printed about 20 times.'

Party hard

There are some celebrities, other celebrities bitch, who would attend the opening of a small bag of cocaine.

Every week, in Sydney in particular, there are dozens of product launches, parties and movie premieres. At each one lurks a social photographer, desperately looking for somebody to photograph.

'If the Lord Mayor's doing a New Year's Eve function and you can buy a couple of tickets, go to it,' said Max. 'If Keanu Reeves is coming to the premiere of *Matrix II*, see if you can get there and give him a kiss. Boom! You're on the front pages of papers all over the world.'

Professional guests perform an important commercial function on the party scene. **Public relations** companies are paid pornographic sums of money to ensure their clients win press coverage for the launch of their bar, restaurant or tinea cream. The PR industry — if you can call something that produces nothing an 'industry' — claims a positive story in the press is worth five times the cost of an advertisement (ten times if the client is a bank) and writes its bills accordingly.

If nobody worth photographing attends an event, no pictures appear in the Sunday papers and the PR's poodle has to go without fillet steak for a week.

Dress to impress (the photographers)

Bessie, whose fame stems from her founding an agency for big-breasted body models, said, 'The company got a lot of press, then it was a matter of the events we were going to. We'd always turn up not too far away from the time we were invited, about half an hour late, and looking the part. There was a party for a health magazine and on the invite there was a chilli, so I got this dress made up out of chillies.'

Former SBS sports presenter Mieke Buchan, who is best known for attending things, once attended the premiere of surfing movie *Blue Crush* in a halter top and sarong, with a hibiscus in her hair, then slipped out of the cinema as the film started, changed and raced off to a Fox TV party, where she was photographed in a different — but equally appropriate — outfit.

Get papped

According to Bessie, Mieke told her, 'Every time I'm in the papers, it's an income-raiser for me.' It makes her better known, which means she is invited to more functions, becomes paid to attend functions and ultimately becomes the object of functions, at which she comes to wonder who is the grinning stranger[1] standing next to her.

A good way to get your picture in the papers is to appear to want not to be photographed, and to be hounded by the paparazzi. The paparazzi do not always know who to hound, so it helps if you let them know you don't want to be snapped, and exactly where you will be when you don't want your picture taken.

'There is a certain type of celebrity who will get someone else — ie, their agent — to tip off the pap photographers that they will be at a certain restaurant, beach or party,' said Louisa Hatfield, editorial director of celebrity gossip weeklies *NW* and *Woman's Day* (where I worked for six months, in another lifetime). 'The pap photographers will go along, and there they will be — and isn't it a coincidence that they're having a record launch the next day?'

---

[1] It's probably Richard Branson.

Get surgery

Bondi Beach in summer is a seaside celebration of sand and salt, much of which can be found in the silicone and saline implants of models and cable-TV presenters.

'I never suggest anyone has a boob job,' said Bessie. 'There were so many girls in our agency who had fake ones anyway that natural boobs became a commodity that was really hard to get hold of.' Boom-boom.

On 'a few rare occasions', Bessie has proposed surgery. 'One girl came in for a meeting and she had this really large nose,' she said. 'I said, "Have you ever thought about getting a nose job?" She said, "I've just had one!" With nose jobs, they take a while to settle down.'

'God sometimes is cruel,' said Martin Bedford, of theatrical agents Bedford & Pearce. 'Other times, he is extra kind. There are some people who look fantastic — other people need maybe slight adjustments.'

Surgical procedures Martin might recommend to his clients include the removal of large birthmarks and eye realignment.

'If both eyes are staring at their nose, they're not going to be looking at the audience,' he pointed out.

If your operation goes wrong, you can always console yourself with the thought that you will appear on one of *NW*'s regular 'Cosmetic Surgery Disasters' covers.

Get onto reality TV

Reality TV offers people a new type of fame, unconnected with accomplishment. It is a fame that comes suddenly, brutally and frighteningly, then disappears. One day, everybody in the country knows who you are, the next day your mother calls you by all your siblings' — and cousins' — names before she gets to yours.

There are two A-lists in Australia. The first is headed by the male Packers and other unattractive multimillionaires who never get photographed at parties. The second is the province of the attractive young super-rich — such as Sarah Murdoch — and the reality TV stars. As soon as reality TV stars are thrown off their shows, everybody wants to meet them.

A former resident of *The Block* (the reality TV show, not the predominantly Aboriginal area of Redfern, Sydney) Phil Rankine told me, 'Just after *The Block*, we went to two or three [functions] a week.' He and his wife, Amity Dry, met Sarah Murdoch, Ian Thorpe, Richard Wilkins — 'real A-list stuff' — but, he said, 'The funny thing was, we'd meet up with all the *Big Brother* people. We kind of knew them [from watching them on TV] and they knew us — but we didn't know each other.

'Celebrities have seen the show like everyone else,' said Phil. 'I was at the ARIA awards, and I went up to [double-platinum-selling pop star] Alex Lloyd to say hi, and he went, "My God! Phil! I've got to grab my wife!"'

People used to be fascinated by TV stars because they had more interesting lives than TV viewers — but the *Big Brother* housemates have less interesting lives than practically anyone in Australia. They do not go to work, they do not go shopping, they do not leave the house. They cannot even join in the national conversation about reality TV: when the stars of *The Block* met the *Big Brother* evictees in a Bondi street, the now-forgotten former housemate Patrick was perhaps the only person in Sydney's eastern suburbs who did not recognise the now-forgotten Amity Dry — he had been stuck for weeks in a house without a television.

The old, merit-based kind of celebrity, by which people were famous for running four-minute miles, or being elected prime minister, or balancing the largest number of eggs on their nose, was divisive and undemocratic. There was a feeling that not everybody was in with the same chance. Many did not have the speed, or the numbers in caucus, or a big enough nose. With reality TV, such considerations no longer apply. Now we have a democracy of celebrity. We could all do what reality TV stars do. If there were any measure of how to do it well, we could probably do it better than they do.

Get a lifestyle

The prime-time popularity of 'lifestyle TV' — at the expense of drama and comedy — has warped the lives of conventional agents and actors. Martin Bedford represents Holly Brisley, a conventionally gorgeous TV presenter and actor whose appearance on the cover pushed sales of *Ralph* past 100,000 for the first time.

I spoke to him before she broke in to *Home and Away*, when her career seemed to be sadly stalled.

'There's not a great deal for people like Holly to do,' said Martin. 'Her drama career is a bit on hold, because we don't have American-style dramas here at the moment. Some of our TV series have been cut, *White Collar Blue* has gone, and everybody wants people to be Jamie Oliver or a gardener or whatever. Every week, I get 20 calls for "somebody like Jamie Oliver".

'We've got a lot of people who can cook — I have French chefs, I have girl chefs — but I don't have another Jamie Oliver. A lot of the time producers have in their mind exactly what they want. Skilled presenters, skilled actors such as Holly, who actually mould characters and put them together, [lose out because] once again, reality TV has come into casting.'

Holly Brisley is regularly at parties and in the social pages. 'It helps to keep your face out there,' she told me, 'but when you're at too many of them, it often means you're not working.'

Martin said, 'Holly's the sort of girl I can say to: "Holly, you're auctioning tomorrow, you're jumping out of a plane the next day, then you're going into an arena at the rugby final and running around in a barrel." Holly will do anything you ask of her. She's not frightened. Everything is a challenge, and she just wants to succeed.'

The weekend before we spoke, Martin told me, 'Holly and Sister2Sister and Russell Crowe's band, the Grunts, were playing on a field in Darling Harbour, for Vodaphone. It was good fun, a nice social occasion, and, hey presto!, she's in the *Tele on Sunday*.'

And she was singing?

'No, no.'

She was dancing?

'Holly was actually playing rugby.'

The teams were one girl short.

'Mieke Buchan couldn't go that night,' Martin explained.

Make a sex tape

You want to be on the big screen but you are not being offered those starring roles? Why not make a video of yourself having sex? Whether you like it or not, it will soon be shown at sports clubs and bucks nights throughout the country, if not the world.

The fashion for celebrity sex videos began in the US, with a tape of actor Rob Lowe and two women in a hotel room, but the most famous example is the stolen video of Pamela Anderson and Tommy Lee's honeymoon, complete with not-very-interesting footage of Tommy fishing.

The first Australian victim of sex tape theft was Mimi Macpherson: a 1997 video of her with then boyfriend Matthew Bennett was more watched than the footy grand final. In 1998, beleaguered singer Debra Byrne became the second victim: a tape of her and her former lover Chris Bekker was stolen from her home. A certain former *Home and Away* star not mentioned elsewhere in this book and her partner appear in another feature widely available from adult video shops.

And, of course, we will always have Paris.

There are so many celebrity sex videos, they have become a new cinematic genre, with their own narrative conventions (the heroine always appears to be drunk) and hand-held video camera cinematography. Innovatively, the Paris Hilton video appears to be filmed through a khaki filter, lending the action a retro, 'wartime' feel.

Lose it

Give your sex tape a discreet title, such as *Me and Rick as XXX Porn Stars*, and leave it somewhere safe, such as the middle of the coffee table at a Christmas party. Even better, give it to your ex-partner as something to remember you by. It will be available on-line faster than you can say, 'It's just a model who looks like me. With, um, another model who looks like him.'

Celebrities are criminally careless with their sex tapes, always returning them to the video shop by mistake, or leaving them in the VCR when the rellos come around.

When Pamela and Tommy's sex video was stolen, the couple produced their own edit, copyrighted it and marketed it, but most celebrities are mortified by the exposure. Debra Byrne was devastated when her video was stolen. The burglar was caught but the tape had already been pirated. Chris Bekker then accepted $10,000 from *New Idea* to talk about his pain and shame.

Have a diet crisis or a fat hell

'I believe every single person in the world has got an angle on them,' said Max Markson.

'If they're fat, maybe they're the fattest person in Australia, or they're the most slovenly, or they've got the dirtiest house, or they're going to try to lose the most weight in the next six months.'

Louisa Hatfield told me *NW*'s top-selling covers of the year are always its 'body-image' covers. Stars who would not ordinarily appear in *NW* — which, said Louisa, 'apart from reality TV, is very Hollywood focused' — can shift thousands of copies if they undergo a sudden, dramatic shape change.

'Kirstie Alley has worked on *NW* because she became so ... enormous,' said Louisa. 'In size. Her battle with her weight [she reached 130 kilograms] has been hugely empowering for the readers.'

Britney Spears got a cover for growing too big, and Nicole Richie for becoming too skinny.

Former reality TV stars tend to have a shelf life slightly shorter than that of strawberries. Will any of the latest punnet still be on magazine covers next year?

'If they get incredibly fat or thin, they can get on any time,' said Louisa.

Afterword

Bastards have infiltrated society at every level. They run the government, the corporate so-called world, international terrorism, a number of catering businesses and the sport of golf. They have coaxed us into speaking their language, and mummified our dreams in Post-it notes and defaced our hopes with fridge magnets.

It is time to fight back.

But how?

Well, you've taken the first step by buying this book. Your next step might be to buy several more copies of this book, and give them to your friends and family. A third step might be to include casual acquaintances in the wider circle of people for whom you buy this book. Once your local shops have sold out, you could begin to explore other options. You might be able to find extra copies on the internet, for example.

Only when you have exhausted every possible opportunity to make me a wealthier, more successful author will you know it is time to take the fight to the enemy.

The important thing to remember is we must not simply descend to their level. We must sink far, far lower. We must hit the bastards where it hurts — in the office. We must leave small, dead animals in their in-trays. We must send obscene emails from their terminals. We must steal their SIM cards and text message death threats to their superiors. We must draw weeping penises on their whiteboards, insert images of farmyard porn in their PowerPoint presentations, and saw through the strap on their messenger bags.

As I hinted in the introduction, I believe there should be a short annual season for bastard-hunting. It would run from, say, the end of the financial year on June 30 to Chainsaw Al Dunlap's birthday on July 26. During this time, it would be legal to shoot bastards with shotguns or pursue them with hounds, provided there were no objections from the landowners over whose fields the bastards might trespass during the course of the chase.

There is ample evidence that bastards would actually benefit from this humane method of keeping down their numbers, and would probably stop stealing farmers' chickens, too.

We can also fight back by making small changes in our own lives. Each time we suppress the desire to draw quotation marks in the air, we strike a blow against bastardry. Each time we refuse to use a noun as a verb, a sporting term as a metaphor, or a junior employee as a punching bag, we undermine their power.

This book may be small but perfectly formed, but it is only the first chapter. The future is unwritten.

About the Author

Mark Dapin is the author of *Sex & Money*, a memoir of the time he spent working on men's magazines. He is a features writer and fortnightly columnist on *Good Weekend* magazine in the *Sydney Morning Herald* and *The Age*. He is one of only two people in the world to have worked for both *Ralph* and the *Australian Financial Review*.

He was born in the UK, but moved to Australia in 1989. Apart from a couple of years in the print industry, he has been a journalist all his working life. Before that, he was a hopeless failure.

He has two degrees and is studying for two more. By an unusual quirk of fate, Mark has no star sign.

Acknowledgments

Parts of this book originally appeared as columns in *Good Weekend* magazine.

Thanks to *Good Weekend*'s editor, Judith Whelan, for giving me a regular platform to rant and ramble, and censoring nothing beyond gratuitous profanity.

Thanks to *Good Weekend*'s previous editor, Fenella Souter, for giving me an irregular platform some years earlier.

Thanks to *Good Weekend*'s sub-editors, for picking up innumerable factual errors in the original columns (although I've put back all the jokes you cut out).

Also thanks to Amruta and Patrick, and shots out to all my homies in lock down.